Historical Sketches
of Ottawa

Historical Sketches of Ottawa

Leslie Maitland

drawings by
Louis Taylor

Broadview Press
Peterborough, Ontario
1990
First Printing

Canadian Cataloguing in Publication Data

Maitland, Leslie
    Historical Sketches of Ottawa

ISBN 0-921149-67-0

1. Historic buildings - Ontario - Ottawa.
2. Architecture - Ontario - Ottawa.
3. Ottawa (Ont.) - Buildings,
    structures, etc.
I. Taylor, Louis A. (Louis Albert), 1950-
II. Title.

FC3096.7.M34 1990   971.3'84   C90-094886-8
F1059.5.09M34 1990

broadview press
P.O. Box 1243
Peterborough, Canada. K9J 7H5

in the U.S.:
broadview press
421 Center St.
Lewiston, N.Y. 14092

Printed and bound in Canada by
Gagne Ltd.

Table of contents

To my parents and my husband

Preface

Ottawa the capital city. Most visitors come to the capital to see the Parliament Buildings, museums, monuments and other structures that bear witness to Ottawa's role as the nation's capital. But there is another city here as well. It is a residential, commercial, industrial and religious city. It is to be found on shady residential avenues, on busy, commercial streets, around the corner from the great monuments, or in outlying areas.

This book is an introduction — and only an introduction — to Ottawa's historic architecture. Within the constraints of this volume, we have chosen the year 1900 as our cut-off date, and this explains why many fine buildings — such as the new Centre Block of the Parliament Buildings (begun in 1917) are not included. Also excluded are some nineteenth century buildings that have been so heavily modified that they no longer can be considered buildings of their time: for this reason we illustrate Rideau Hall Gatehouse, but not Rideau Hall itself, which is more a structure of the twentieth century than the nineteenth.

If you use this book as a walking tour, feel free to follow it in any order that suits you. You will find that the texts are written in a manner that allows you to dip into it at any point, and for this reason some of the background information is repeated. It was difficult to limit our choice to the sixty-odd buildings that this volume allows, since there are so many fine buildings in the city of Ottawa. Those shown here are just a few of our favourites. We hope, while you are wandering the streets of Ottawa during your visit, you will discover some favourites of your own, too.

Several people have assisted me in the production of this book. I would particularly like to thank Michael Newton, Senior Planner, Heritage and Capital History, National Capital Commission; and Stuart Lazear, Senior Heritage Planner, City of Ottawa, both of whom have allowed me free access to their files. David Bulloch, archivist for the City of Ottawa, and Brian Hallett, archivist, National Archives, were both extremely helpful. I would also like to thank my colleagues at the Architectural History Branch of the Canadian Parks Service: Jacqueline Adell, Margaret Coleman, Sally Coutts, Mary Cullen, Marc deCaraffe, James DeJonge, Ian Doull, Jule Harris, Robert Hunter, Dana Johnson, Kate MacFarlane, Joan Mattie, Martha Phemister, Shannon Ricketts, C. James Taylor, and Janet Wright. Special thanks to my husband, J. Daniel Livermore, who edited this manscript.

Introduction

The City in the Nineteenth Century

The nation's capital: today, this is every Canadian's idea of Ottawa, and this is its significance to the rest of the country. The visitor to the National Capital Region (which is the name given to Ottawa, Hull and the surrounding countryside) sees beautifully laid-out parks, handsomely designed and interesting museums, the Parliament Buildings, the War Memorial, government offices, embassies and official residences — in short, all the accoutrements of a national capital. Ottawa is a handsome city, and a source of pride to all Canadians.

Ottawa was once a very different place. From the beginning of the last century until its end, this location has been an Indian campsite, a lumbertown, a milltown, a military encampment, a provincial capital, and finally a national capital. Even after Ottawa was named the capital of Canada it remained very much a centre of industry and commerce, and it was not until the close of the nineteenth century that government overtook industry as the city's major concern.

Each stage of Ottawa's development has been the result of geographic necessity. Samuel de Champlain stopped off here in 1613 during his westerly explorations. He was impressed with the beauty of the place and gave the name Rideau (curtain) to the lovely plummeting sheet of water that joins the Rideau River with the Ottawa. Long before the arrival of the French, Ottawa had been the jumping off point for canoes headed west through the interior towards Georgian Bay. After the French came, commerce increased along this river as the heavily laiden canoes — headed west full of trade goods to exchange for the furs that would fill the canoes for the return trip east to Montreal and subsequently to Europe — negotiated the Chaudière (meaning kettle in French, for the water seems to boil over the rocks) Falls. Nothing tangible remains of these two centuries of activity beyond a few archaeological remains. But looking at the broad and fast Ottawa River, the Chaudière and Rideau Falls, the cliffs that frame the outlet of the Rideau Canal, the forest that rises in the distance to the north, one can still appreciate the wild and rugged place that this once was.

Development in this area began in the early part of the nineteenth century with the exploitation of the Ottawa Valley timber stands. The Ottawa Valley and the Laurentian Shield which rises on both sides of it were once covered with dense forests of valuable timber, especially white and red pine. This was the primeval forest: trees of awesome size hundreds of years old, cut to feed Britain's insatiable appetite for the timber that was needed to build her fleets during the Napoleonic Wars. Beginning in 1806 the first timber rafts slid down river to Montreal where they were loaded onto ships for the trans-Atlantic crossing. For another hundred years, timber remained the basis of the Ottawa economy and the foundation of many local fortunes.

Geographic considerations entered once again into the course of the city's history in 1815, when Canada concluded three years of war with the United States. It was an uneasy peace, and fearful of more Yankee aggression, the British government sought to secure lines of communication from Lower Canada (now Quebec) to Upper Canada (now Ontario). The water route along the St. Lawrence River between Montreal and Kingston was vulnerable to attack from the south, and so a route around had to be created. In 1826, Lieutenant Colonel John By of the Royal Engineers began construction of a canalized waterway to run 123 miles, through 47 locks, from the confluence of the Rideau and Ottawa Rivers to Kingston. This was one of the greatest episodes in Canadian history: hundreds of men battled forest, swamp, insects, malaria, dysentry, violence and loneliness to construct what was then the most significant engineering project in the world. Upon termination in 1832, at the cost of many lives and over one million pounds sterling, the Rideau Canal was the longest canalized waterway in the world

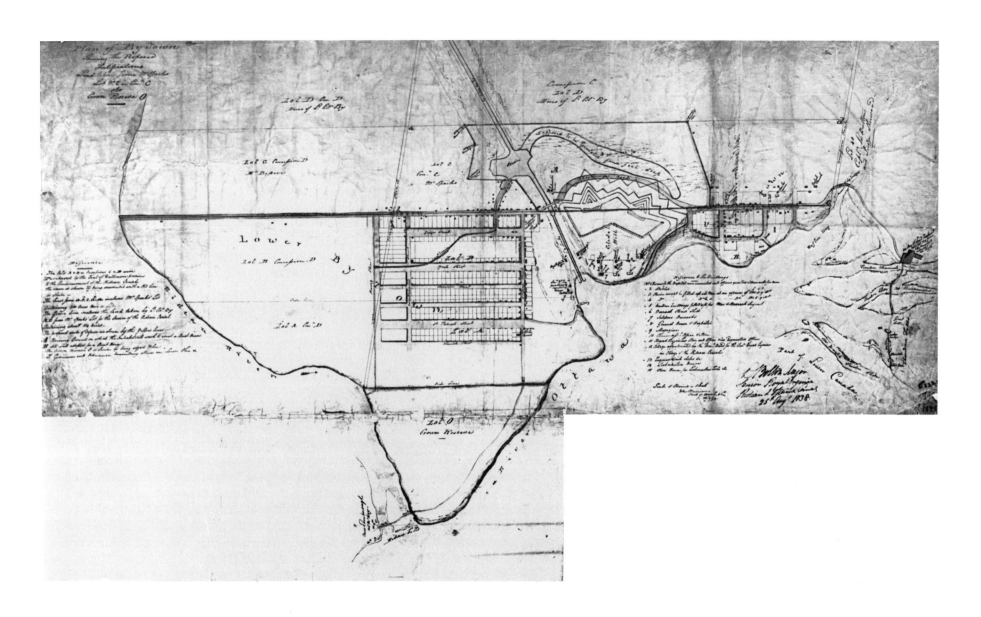

Bytown as a military encampment, 1838. Note the entrance to the
canal flanked by a fortified hill (Barrack Hill, now Parliament Hill)
and the neatly laid out streets of Bytown.
(National Archives, Map Collection, NMC 18913)

and included the world's two highest dams (at Jones Falls and Hog's Back).

The long-awaited American invasion never came, but the canal proved its worth as a transportation link through the interior of the province, which was opened up for settlement and development. Steamboats plied the waterway, serving the communities along its course, well into this century. The village at the northern end of the canal was named Bytown in honour of the man whose work here coalesced the scattered settlements in the area into a place with a sense of identity. By laid out the townsite, organized the Byward market, and set the Board of Ordnance (a unit of the British army) the task of civil administration.

During the construction of the canal, a Scottish stonemason named Thomas MacKay came to this area, and he quickly recognized the potential of the Rideau River. He purchased eleven hundred acres on both sides of the mouth of the River from its confluence with the Ottawa and running south. Upon this stretch of river he erected lumber mills, cloth mills, flour mills and grist mills. The power of the river ran his industries and brought workers to settle in the area, particularly in New Edinburgh (named for MacKay's home in Scotland). They were soon joined in the area by farmers, timber cutters, and all the tradesmen who were needed to supply a growing community.

The Rideau waterway was defended by a military encampment on the cliffs high above the eight locks that join the canal with the Ottawa River. The military

The Parliament Buildings and the lumbertown, circa 1866. (National Archives, C 1185)

encampment and the presence of large numbers of soldiers, together with labourers from the canal, the mills and the lumber camps formed the character of the town at mid-century. It was a rough place. Heavy drinking, rowdyism, sectarian conflict and civil disturbances characterized life in this pioneer town. Gradually, civil authority took over from the Board of Ordnance to cope with the growth of the area and with its needs. The village of Bytown was incorporated in 1850. By mid-century, Bytown was a well-established, lively industrial centre which attracted new businesses. On Christmas Day in 1854, the first train arrived, linking Bytown with Montreal and Pembroke. In 1855 Bytown was incorporated as a city and Bytown was renamed Ottawa, a name considered more dignified.

Bytown would probably have remained a bustling little frontier town were it not for geography. Sitting as it did on the border between Canada East (as Lower Canada had been called since 1841) and Canada West (Upper Canada, now Ontario), Bytown came to the attention of the colonial government as a suitable site for the government of the United Province of Canada. The government had alternated between Toronto and Quebec City, and all the moving and disruption made for a highly unsatisfactory arrangement. Bytown had the advantage of being on the border of the two provinces, while not being one of the cities so vigorously (even violently) promoted by their respective citizens. Bytown was designated the new capital in 1857.

In 1859, construction began on four buildings to serve the new government: a parliament building, a parliamentary library, and two buildings for the various government departments. The site chosen was the military encampment overlooking the Rideau locks and the Ottawa River. But even as the capital of the United Canadas was beginning to take form, a movement was afoot to create an independent nation not just of Quebec and Ontario, but of the Maritime colonies as well. Confederation brought the Dominion of Canada

into existence on July 1, 1867, and the capital of the United Provinces became the capital of the new nation.

The nature of Ottawa's development began to change after 1867. Lumbering and milling remained significant in the city's economy, but gradually Ottawa became a government town. New suburbs in Sandy Hill and the Glebe opened up for the civil servants who took up residence here. The Byward market enlarged and improved, hotels became more gracious, and shopping districts were rebuilt with handsome structures. There was a perception that as a capital city, Ottawa ought to have some civil amenities such as parks and boulevards and handsome public structures. These began to appear here and there, on a piece-meal basis. It was not, however, until the Laurier government (1896-1911) that a concerted plan was drawn up to beautify the city. But that is the story of the next century.

Architecture in Ottawa in the Nineteenth Century

Ottawa's nineteenth century buildings reflect trends in architectural development current throughout British North America, while certain local conditions gave the city's architecture its individual flavour. During the first half of the century, architecture was dominated by European classicism. Architecture of classical inspiration has generally low, horizontal proportions, symmetrical facades, roofs of a moderate pitch, evenly spaced door and window openings, and sometimes certain classical details such as columns, pediments, fanlights, and mouldings based upon antique Greek and Roman precedent. This theme had persisted in western architecture since the Renaissance, and it was this style of architecture that the French and then the British brought to the New World.

While this architectural style ruled public building and work done by professional architects, it also formed the basis of so-called vernacular design. In buildings

Bird's eye view of Ottawa, the emerging capital. This watercolour probably dates from the 1860s.

grand and humble, the principles of classical design ruled all. It was an architecture of subtle grace which gave great dignity even to the most modest structure.

In the Ottawa buildings that survive to this day, this classicism is clearly expressed. We see it in fine buildings such as the Bingham-McKellar House, Maplelawn, the Donnelly House and the Billings Estate. We see vernacular classicism also expressed more modestly in smaller structures such as the Heney House, 71 Thomas, and the Fraser Schoolhouse.

All these buildings, however, are very distinctly Ottawa valley structures in their materials, builders, and designs. The delicately tinted grey stone is the local limestone, and the men who built these houses were the same skilled stonemasons of Scottish and Irish descent who built the Rideau Canal. The thick walls and relatively small window openings of these buildings are in response to the severity of Ottawa winters. Steep roofs, casement windows and front verandahs are features of French Canadian architecture.

By mid-century the tradition of classical architecture was about to change dramatically, in Ottawa as throughout the Western world. These changes affected design, materials and the siting on streets; they affected the types of buildings constructed, the ways they were built and used; they affected heat, light, water supply, sewage disposal — in short, the second half of the nineteenth century witnessed a revolution in architecture.

The most visually obvious change was in design. Tired of the unchanging qualities of classical design, architects rummaged through the attics of European historical architecture in search of freshness and variety. One by one a host of new historical revival styles came into favour: the Italianate, Romanesque Revival, Second Empire, Gothic Revival and Queen Anne Revival styles. In reviving styles of previous centuries for modern use, architects adapted these styles to modern tastes. Buildings were now meant to be picturesque; that is, they were artfully arranged compositions of verticals and horizontals, projections and recessions, steeply pitched roofs, high chimneys, handsome carving and architectural details, and beautiful materials. Such houses were meant to be seen in prettily-laid out and very English gardens. They satisfied the Victorian taste for variety and interest.

Many of these changes in design were made possible by changes in spheres of interest outside of architecture. Railway construction across the continent and improved trans-Atlantic travel made it possible to import materials from one area to another: one could have brick from southern Ontario, slate from the Eastern Townships, stone from the Maritimes, tiles from Holland, stained glass from England, and so on. Ideas, too, came with the new generation of architects emigrating from Great Britain, and with the architectural publications that contained illustrations of fashionable design.

Changes in engineering affected the design of furnaces, making it possible to eliminate the cast iron stove and the dangerous and inefficient open fireplace. Someone thought of plumbing; waterworks were built and the privy moved indoors. Glass manufacture became more sophisticated, so that there was a greater choice of window types possible. Woodworking tools became more mechanized, so that more and more houses, even those of humble character, could have handsome mouldings, ordered pre-cut from the lumber-yard instead of laboriously cut by hand. Brick was cast in uniform sizes and fired in ovens of more even heat, so that it became a much more desirable construction material. Plaster, paint, tile and virtually every other material used in construction improved in quality and became more available to a wider group of consumers.

The result for Ottawa was an architecture that in the second half of the nineteenth century bore little relation to that of the first. Ottawa architecture was rather more like architecture elsewhere in the country: picturesque and eclectic, with more attention paid to the creature comforts. Architecture and the city of Ottawa grew hand in hand. The Court House, Parliament Buildings, Registry Office, Waterworks and fashionable suburban house: each reflects the tastes and constructional techniques of its times.

The Sketches

1

The Eight Locks and Commissariat Building

Colonel By Valley
1826-32

Our story begins on the bridge between the Parliament Buildings and the Chateau Laurier. Here there is a twisting stair that invites you to walk down: take the time to explore this little valley carefully. Later on your walk about town, look back towards the valley from Nepean Point or from the grounds of the Museum of Civilization, and admire the beauty of the little ravine tucked into a cleft in the cliffs. This shady valley is the cradle of Ottawa.

Between 1812 and 1815 the United States waged war against Great Britain, and the focus of the attack was the colonies of British North America. Britain fought the war at a great disadvantage: the armaments, most supplies, and many of the soldiers had to be imported from England. Once in Lower Canada, everyone and everything had to be shipped to the scene of the fighting far inland in Upper Canada, along the St. Lawrence River and along the Niagara frontier. The St. Lawrence River was at that time cut in many places by fast and treacherous rapids, requiring that boats be off-

loaded and everything portaged around the rapids to the next sheet of smooth water. It was a slow and expensive trip. Worse, it was dangerous: the St. Lawrence was vulnerable to attack from the south.

Eventually the war was concluded, but it was an uneasy peace. Mindful of the weaknesses of their supply routes, the British Army determined to create an alternative route to avoid the exposed jugular of the St. Lawrence from Montreal to Kingston. After an initial survey and consideration of various possibilities, it was eventually decided to construct a canalized waterway (that is, linking existing rivers and lakes) from Kingston along the Cataraqui River, joining the Rideau River at its confluence with the Ottawa River. The task turned out to be much greater than anyone imagined.

In 1826 Lieutenant Colonel John By (1779-1836) commenced work on the canal at a narrow slit between these cliffs. A member of the Corps of Royal Engineers and a graduate of the Royal Military Academy at Woolwich, By was a seasoned veteran and had seen service in the Peninsular Wars. The first part of the project was the most difficult: in this location, locks had to be built to overcome an eighty foot rise of land from the Ottawa River to a beaver meadow above. The eight locks were to be part of a larger complex of military structures. To defend the locks from attack, army barracks and an army hospital sat upon what is now Parliament Hill. On the opposite slope were the houses of By and other officials attached to the project.

All that remains of the complex are the locks themselves and the Commissariat Building, which is the lower of the two buildings along the locks. It is a simple, masonry structure. Built as an office, treasury, and storehouse for material needed on the project, the Commissariat was erected in 1827 and is the oldest surviving structure in the city core of Ottawa. This building is now the Bytown Museum and is well worth a visit. The upper building is the Lockmaster's Station. It was built in 1888 of roughcast masonry, in a picturesque design

meant to harmonize with the rustic setting. All of the stone used in the locks and the buildings was quarried from the nearby cliffs.

A project of such magnitude attracted many businesses to provision the site. Soon carpenters, shoemakers, tailors, bakers, butchers and many others had established themselves on the nearby height of land. By had a proper townsite surveyed, and the Board of Ordnance found itself responsible for the running of a busy little settlement that called itself Bytown in honour of its creator.

In May of 1832 the steamship Rideau officially opened the waterway. Once finished, the waterway was 200 kilometers long and included 47 locks, 14 dams, and the world's two highest dams at Hog's Back and Jones Falls. It was the world's longest canalized waterway, and was the most ambitious project that the British government had ever undertaken in any of its colonies. But it was not without cost. Labouring through dense forest, battling mosquitoes, blackflies, bad water, and crude building techniques, many labourers lost their lives through disease and accident. By himself was a victim of the project. He was recalled to London to explain why the project had cost 1 million pounds — far more than had been originally estimated — to people who could not possibly have understood the difficulties of construction through bush, swamp, rock, and Canadian winters. His career slid into a sad eclipse and he died prematurely at the age of 56.

Although never needed for defence, the waterway quickly proved its worth as a transportation route. With access to markets assured, farmers, millers and lumbermen opened up the interior for settlement between Ottawa and Kingston. The waterway was an important commercial route well into the 20th century, when it was finally superceded by rail and highway travel. Today the waterway is busier than it has ever been, drawing thousands of tourists a year from all around the world.

2, 3, 4
East Block
Library of Parliament
Parliamentary Fence

View of the East Block tower taken from Elgin Street, with the original Centre Block in the background.
(National Archives)

From the protected trench of the Rideau Canal, it is only a short walk up the gentle incline of Wellington Street to the precincts of Parliament Hill, one of Canada's most famous and recognizable landmarks and the site of perhaps the most ambitious architectural undertaking in Canadian history.

By the 1850s political fortune was about to smile on Ottawa, for reasons which had little to do with the city's economy or reputation. Since the burning of the parliament buildings in Montreal in 1849, the United Province of Canada (present-day Ontario and Quebec) had had a "rotating capital", alternating between Toronto and Quebec every two years. It was a system with built-in inefficiencies, and every Canadian political leader knew that a permanent capital was needed. But because of sectional and regional rivalries, and the tight division between Reformers and Conservatives in this period, no government could tackle the issue successfully. Finally in 1856, John A. Macdonald, then Attorney-General West and leader of the Upper Canadian Conservatives, pushed through the legislature a motion that Queen Victoria should select the permanent capital of Canada.

Governor General Sir Edmund Head played a decisive role by submitting to the Queen a memorandum arguing the merits of Ottawa as an ideal compromise choice. In 1857, the Queen reached her decision, and a year later the Government announced plans to build three parliamentary buildings on the ordnance lands high above the Rideau Canal.

The Government wasted little time in launching a competition to design and construct the parliament buildings. Using a landscape design by Samuel Keefer, Deputy-Commissioner of Public Works, notices announcing the competition called for plans for three buildings on Barrack Hill: a central parliamentary building with an attached library; and two Departmental Buildings on the East and West flanks, which would house virtually all of the fledgling public service of the province.

Eighteen architectural firms submitted twenty-three separate designs for the complex of three buildings, and all designs were evaluated against ten criteria. Toronto architects Fuller and Jones won the competition for the parliamentary or centre block and the library, while the partnership of Thomas Stent and Augustus Laver, English-trained architects from Ottawa, won first prize for designs of the East and West Blocks. Late in 1859, tenders were issued and contracts were awarded to the Quebec City firm of Thomas McGreevy, who subsequently divided the contract, giving the Departmental buildings to the firm of Jones, Haycock and Company of Port Hope.

Excavation on the site began in December, 1859, but construction of the complex was a long and contentious process. Design changes were necessary at the outset of construction, and both the East and West Blocks changed in appearance, thereby ceasing to be twin buildings. The exterior walls were changed to "Nepean sandstone", which created a polychromatic or multi-coloured appearance, one of the complex's most pleasing architectural effects.

Rising costs were the project's most difficult problem. By 1861 the parliamentary appropriation was exhausted with the buildings barely above the foundations, and a Royal Commission of Enquiry was called to examine the many irregularities of the construction project. In 1863 with new architects in charge, construction began afresh, although work on the parliamentary library was suspended until the 1870s, when more funds became available. In the fall of 1865 the first occupants moved onto Parliament Hill, and in practical terms Ottawa became the capital of the Province of Canada.

Now only the East Block, the Library and the Parliamentary Fence remain in their essentially original conditions. The Centre Block burned to the ground in 1916 and was re-constructed in the 19teens and 20s based upon newer construction techniques and a more modern design. The Parliamentary Library survived the

fire and has been preserved in its original design. The West Block was modified several times over the course of a century, once following a major fire in 1897, and was substantially renovated in the 1950s. Only portions of the exterior resemble the original design of the 1859 competition. The Parliamentary Fence has been modified in keeping with the demands of traffic flow, but retains the essential characteristics of the 1870s in which it was built.

The East Block, the Library of Parliament and the

Library of Parliament.
(National Archives)

Parliamentary Fence, illustrated here, along with the West Block, form one of the most significant monuments of the Gothic Revival style to be found anywhere in the world. The Gothic Revival style had begun almost a century earlier in England, when features of medieval architecture such as the pointed opening, the trefoil and the buttress were introduced as decorative ornaments. Subsequently a more archaeological and scientific approach to the style prevailed, and architects attempted to revive the plans, elevations and decorative schema of medieval buildings for modern use. This complex represents a later and more mature phase in the Gothic Revival. By the mid-nineteenth century, architects were borrowing details and designs from many European countries and from many periods of the middle ages, producing beautiful and imaginative designs.

The Parliament Buildings (including the original Centre Block) were laid out in a manner reminiscent of medieval colleges, around a central quadrant. The East Block in particular is a superb example of the mature Gothic Revival. Based upon the Oxford Museum of Oxford University, the architectural features of the East Block are robust, and the prominent horizontals and verticals help organize the many details of each facade. A rich variety of sculptural details, textured surfaces, and variously coloured building stones make the building endlessly fascinating to examine.

The Library of Parliament is based upon the round chapter houses of medieval architecture. Its construction in what was then a remote lumbertown on the fringes of empire was a remarkable achievement. Stymied by the difficulties of producing a fireproof roof for this building, the architects sent to England for a cast iron frame, which was shipped over and installed on the spot. During the fire that consumed the Centre Block in 1916, a pair of metal fire doors saved the Library from destruction.

The East Block and the Library are both open to the

Entrance Gate.
(National Archives)

public and both are well worth a visit. The principal corridors and offices of the East Block have been restored, including Sir John A. Macdonald's office and the original Privy Council Chamber. The Library is one of the handsomest rooms in the country. Its interior woodwork was designed by an architect on the staff of the Department of Public Works, Frederick J. Alexander.

While the principal work on the Parliament Buildings was completed in the years 1859-65, the task of completing the interior fittings and laying out the grounds took several more years. The stone and iron fence along Wellington Street was built in 1872-74. The fence is a remarkable structure in its own right. In design and in materials, its stone piers echo the architectural style of the buildings. The grounds were originally laid out by the Dominion Chief Architect, Thomas Fuller (architect of the Library and of the original Centre Block) and American landscape architect Calvert Vaux.

Originally the grounds were much more picturesque than they are now, especially around the Library. Here, instead of parking lots, there were winding paths, a greenhouse, a lookout, and a summerhouse. The wildness of the cliffs themselves has been maintained, and one of the best views of Parliament Hill is to be had from across the river.

5

Langevin Block

62 Wellington Street
1883-89

Across the street from Parliament Hill is the Langevin Block, a fine work of architecture that stands out for its superb design and its unusual colour. Originally the three buildings of Parliament Hill contained all of the federal government, its legislators and civil servants alike. But with the entry into Confederation of the western provinces, and with expanding demands on federal government services, the politicians and civil servants outgrew their quarters on the Hill and new premises had to be constructed. This was the first of many off-the-Hill departmental buildings, and it was intended principally for the once-powerful Department of the Interior and Indian Affairs. The building was named in honour of Sir Hector Langevin, a Father of Confederation, who served in the government of Sir John A. Macdonald as Solicitor General, Postmaster General, Secretary of State, Superintendent of Indian Affairs, and Minister of Public Works.

The Langevin Block is one of the finest examples of the Second Empire style in Canada. This style began in France during the reign of Emperor Louis Napoleon III, with the construction of the New Louvre (1852-57). As the Langevin Block illustrates, buildings in the Second Empire style are usually monumental public structures, several storeys high and of considerable length. Their long facades are symmetrical and organized around a series of projecting portions called pavilions. The architectural composition is basically classical: the building is composed vertically into a base, principal and upper storey, each level separated by stringcourses. The details are also classical, and executed in a rich, sculptural manner. There are round-headed windows, pedimented dormers, and prominent cornices. The most singular feature of the Second Empire style, however, is the roof. This steeply pitched superstructure provided for additional usable space in the attic while creating a grand and picturesque roofline for the building. The mansard roof, as it was called, was named for the French architect who made it famous, Francois Mansart (1598-1666).

When the Langevin Block was in the planning stages, there was some thought given to following the architectural style of the Parliament Buildings. Indeed the architect of the Langevin Block, Thomas Fuller, had also been the designer of the original Centre Block. Fuller, curiously enough, had tired of the Gothic and preferred a more up-to-date classical style. Some find the Langevin Block a bit out of step with the Parliament Buildings. But the Second Empire style of the building was in step with the Second Empire style of the financial institutions that once lined the south side of Wellington Street.

Among the subdued grey stone, painted wood and red brick of most of Ottawa's buildings, the olive colour of the stonework of this building stands out. From a New Brunswick quarry, this sandstone was chosen for its unusual colour, durability, and fine grain, which made possible the superb carving on the structure.

The Langevin Block was renovated in the 1970s, and now houses the Privy Council and the offices of the Prime Minister. It has been designated by the City of Ottawa and it is a National Historic Site.

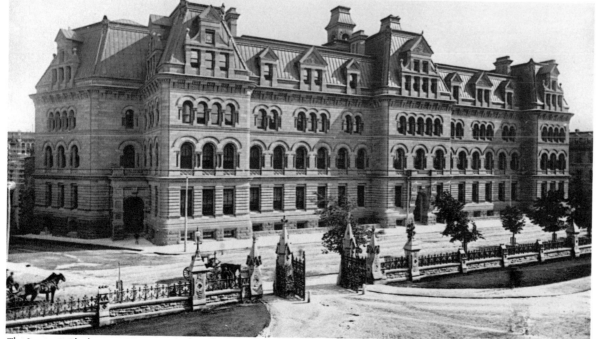

The Langevin Block, circa 1885-90.   (National Archives)

6

Union Bank

128 Wellington Street
1888

F.J. Alexander in 1894.
(National Archives PA 501214)

In 1865 the Union Bank of Lower Canada came into existence. Soon after its incorporation, it expanded its interests outside of Quebec, and became the Union Bank of Canada. In 1871 the Union Bank opened a branch in Ottawa. Construction of a branch office began in 1887 to the designs of Ottawa architect F.J. Alexander, and one year later the bank moved out of its rented quarters into this structure.

The Union Bank has a symmetrical facade of three wide-arched voussoirs surmounted by two storeys elaborately articulated with low-relief sculptural decoration, culminating in a central pediment and abbreviated corner turrets. Stylistically it is a mixture of influences, with Romanesque Revival dominating. The Romanesque Revival was, like the Gothic Revival, a product of the nineteenth century preoccupation with medievalism. Initially, interest in the middle ages was focussed on the pointed arches and delicacy of thirteenth and fourteenth century architecture, but by the mid-nineteenth century, architects and theoreticians turned to the rounded forms and massiveness of twelfth century Romanesque. Rustication, multi-coloured materials, rounded arches, sculptural work and a sense of weight and power characterize this style. The Union Bank is built of New Brunswick sandstone, the same as the Langevin Block at the end of the street. Its lovely olive tint is a handsome contrast to the grey limestone that characterizes so much Ottawa architecture.

Subsequent to the construction of the Parliament Buildings, Wellington Street became the banking centre of the city. Almost all of the south side of the street between the Langevin Block and Bank Street was lined with handsome structures which expressed the wealth and confidence of Canada's banking institutions. All of these former bank buildings are gone, save the former Union Bank.

One by one the banking institutions left their buildings on Wellington Street and the buildings were

Wellington Street in the 1890s.
(National Archives PA 8487)

taken over by government departments. In 1900 the Union Bank moved out of this building, and it was subsequently occupied by the Department of Agriculture, the Ottawa Improvement and Relief Commission, a Commissioner of the North-West Mounted Police, and then, in 1920, the Royal Trust Company moved in. In 1962 the United States Embassy bought the Union Bank with the intention of demolishing it in order to expand their embassy. The federal government prevented this by expropriating the building. It is now rented to the United States Embassy as a storage facility.

Architect Frederick J. Alexander was born in Pewsey, Wiltshire, England in 1849. He studied architecture in London with the firms of J.W. Reed and Lander and Bedells, before emigrating to Canada. He worked briefly for the Toronto firm of Langley, Langley and Burke before coming to Ottawa in 1871 to work for the Department of Public Works. It was while in the offices of the DPW that Alexander designed the Parliamentary fence, and the interior fittings of the Library of Parliament. Between 1877 and 1886 Alexander lived in South Africa, but returned to Ottawa to work in private practice. He died in 1930.

7

St. Andrew's
Presbyterian Church

82 Kent Street
1872-74

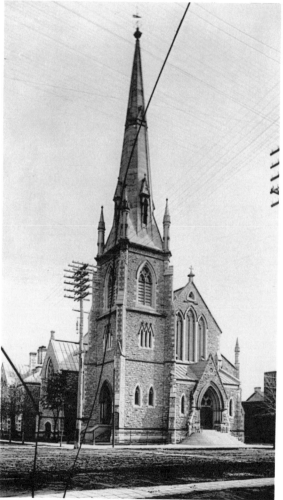

St. Andrew's.
(National Archives)

In the late nineteenth century, a number of congregations in what is now downtown Ottawa demolished their earliest churches, and replaced them with larger and newer buildings designed in more modern tastes. St. Andrew's is among the best of these rebuilt churches. Architecturally the church is a fine adaptation of current trends in Gothic Revival design to local tastes and materials. Here we see the typical church of its era, with a high central nave with intersecting transepts, a one storey porch, and an off-centre tower. Decorative details are sparely used, in accordance with the sober tastes of the Scots Presbyterian parishioners. The few details added to the building are beautifully executed. Note in particular the fine carving around the main door. The building is constructed of Ottawa Valley limestone, heavily rusticated to give the building a greater sense of weight and dignity. The interior has a similarly restrained, yet handsome decorative program.

This church replaced an earlier St. Andrew's Kirk which had been built on this site in 1828, and enlarged in 1855. The foundation stone of the present building was laid in 1872, and by 1874 the new building, designed by architect William T. Thomas, was opened.

Her Royal Highness, Princess Juliana of the Netherlands, donated a handsome lectern to the church, to mark the baptism of her daughter, Princess Magriet Francisca, who was born in Ottawa during the Second World War.

A church hall was erected in 1894 behind the church. After a fire gutted the hall in the 1960s, it was decided to tear down the remaining walls, and erect a modern office building, which contains new church offices, on the land behind the church.

8

Christ Church Anglican Cathedral

439 Queen Street
1872-73

Interior of Christ Church Anglican Cathedral, 1954.
(City of Ottawa Archives)

At first most English-speaking settlers in the Ottawa area took up residence on the north side of the river in what is now Hull. An Anglican church was built there, and it was not until 1833 that an Anglican church was built on the Ottawa side on land donated by Nicholas Sparks, the original owner of much of the land in downtown Ottawa. This first church on the Ottawa side was a modest stone structure, and with the rapid growth of Ottawa after 1867 it was strained beyond capacity. Numerous enlargements were made until it was finally decided to raze the church and replace it with the present edifice. Work began in 1872 and the formal opening was held on 29 September, 1873.

Christ's Church, as it was originally called, was designed by architect King Arnoldi, who had assisted Thomas Fuller on the Parliament Buildings. One can readily identify similarities between Christ Church and the government buildings, such as the use of rough cast Nepean sandstone, and the Gothic Revival style of the church. Its design is based upon that of many English parish churches, having a main hall flanked by low aisles, a side tower and entrance, stepped gables, pointed openings, and prominent end windows to accommodate stained glass panels. A church bell, font and memorial tablet inside were saved from the original structure.

In 1896 the Diocese of Ottawa was created and one year later Christ's Church was renamed Christ Church Cathedral. Cathedrals are necessarily more complex structures than churches, and therefore require additional facilities inside. In 1932 Ottawa architect A.J. Hazelgrove added a new and enlarged chancel and a transept. The interior was remodelled at this time as well, with some particularly fine carving done by craftsmen from Dundas, Ontario. The adjoining parish hall was built in 1902.

The Cathedral is a beautiful structure inside as well as out, with many interesting tablets, military colours and stained glass windows. It is a popular place for organ recitals. The state funeral of Governor General Vincent Massey was held here in 1968.

Architect King Arnoldi (1843-1904) was another graduate of Thomas Fuller's atelier of draughtsmen at the Department of Public Works. His most significant works were done here in Ottawa, and include St. Alban the Martyr Anglican Church (see Number 37), and the former Great North Western Building, now Canada's Four Corners (see Number 10).

9

Slater Building

177-79 Sparks Street
1894

Brouse Building

181-83 Sparks Street
1893

A.J. Stephens Building

185-87 Sparks Street
1896

Originally the commercial district of the village of Bytown was located in Lowertown (now the Byward Market area). But with the construction of the Parliament Buildings, commerce shifted to the areas south of the Hill. Banks tended to locate on Wellington Street (see the Union Bank, Number 6) while the merchants chose premises on Sparks, Metcalfe, O'Connor and Elgin Streets. These are three good examples of that trend.

The Slater Building was erected in 1894 for Robert and Esther Slater. Esther was the daughter of Nicholas Sparks, upon whose land this section of downtown Ottawa was constructed. The Brouse Building was designed by architect George F. Stalker, for fruit merchant Henry A. Brouse. Last of the group was the Stephens Building, probably designed by architect King Arnoldi for merchant A.J. Stephens. All three buildings have had a multiplicity of tenants and uses.

This trio of buildings illustrates well the delightful variety of late nineteenth century commercial design. Within the confines of small facades, the architects of these buildings created diverse and eclectic structures. The windows are large relative to the area of the wall surfaces, so that the upper storeys are well-lit and airy. Each window surround is handsomely crafted with details drawn from several historical styles. The Slater Building has some rather freely interpreted features of the Romanesque Revival style, such as the squat columns and wide arch on the second floor. The red brick of the Brouse Building is a mixture of Italianate and Romanesque Revival, as is the treatment of the window surrounds. The Stephens Building features an unusual combination of an oriel window set inside the lower half of a tall, arched opening. All three buildings have pressed metal cornices.

The three-storey block was the most common type of commercial structure in the nineteenth century. Three storeys were about as far as anyone was prepared to climb, and commerce had to wait for the invention of the elevator before building taller buildings. Some of the best examples of nineteenth century commercial blocks are to be found in small towns, which have not suffered the more damaging effects of commercial prosperity.

Canada's Four Corners

93 Sparks Street
1871

The land from Wellington to Laurier and from Bronson to Waller had been acquired in 1826 by a farmer and businessman named Nicholas Sparks. He had surveyed his property for building lots, only to have 88 acres of it seized by the Crown for the construction of fortifica-

Great Northwestern Telegraph and Cable Office.
(National Archives)

tions. The fortifications were never built and Sparks eventually got his land back, after a lengthy court battle. But development in the Centretown area was slow, since most commercial activity was located on Rideau and Sussex Streets.

By the 1860s Sparks Street became a significant commercial centre, and fine stone buildings began to replace earlier, less pretentious structures. In 1871 this structure was erected of Ohio and Nepean sandstone. It is three and a half storeys high and originally had a mansard roof set with round-headed stone dormers. The carving on this building is particularly fine. Smooth bands contrast with the rougher material of the walls, and articulate the corners of the buildings and the divisions between the storeys. Look up at the keystones on the second storey: each one is a carved head, each different from the others. The sculptor is thought to have been William Hall Burns, who worked on the sculptural programme of the Parliament Buildings.

93 Sparks Street is an early Ottawa example of the Second Empire Style, similar to the Langevin Block (see Number 5), although this building is on a more modest scale. The Second Empire style was an excellent style for commerce — rich, robust and self-confident. Such a prosperous, extroverted image was the desire of the original owners of this structure, the Montreal Telegraph Company, which leased the building initially to the Merchants' Bank. In 1882 the telegraph company, which had become part of the Great Northwest Telegraph Company, moved in. Subsequently the GNT Company and the building were taken over by the Canadian National Railways. In 1968 the building was sold to the National Capital Commission, which rents it out for commercial purposes.

11

14 Metcalfe Street

14 Metcalfe Street
1882

The land on which this building sits was once part of the original tract purchased by Nicholas Sparks in 1826. After Confederation, Wellington Street, Sparks Street, and the connecting streets became the most sought-after district for banks and commercial institutions in the city. In 1872 the heirs of Nicholas Sparks sold this land to the Montreal Telegraph Company, which subse-

The Molson's Bank, ca. 1901-10.
(William M. Harmer Collection, National Archives)

quently sold the land to McLeod Stewart and William Hodgson in 1881. Stewart, a lawyer and one-time mayor of Ottawa, joined with Hodgson, an architect, to dabble in the real estate market. Hodgson, who sold out his share in the venture to Stewart the very next year, was very likely the architect of this building. In design it is very like Hodgson's other building down the street, the Scottish Ontario Chambers.

After the building was finished in 1882, Stewart rented it to the Union Bank of Lower Canada and to various legal firms. Stewart sold the property in 1892, whereupon it was rented by Molson's Bank, which installed a very interesting mosaic floor on the ground level, featuring the coat-of-arms of the bank. This mosaic may still be seen today. In 1903 the Department of Labour moved into this building, with W.L. Mackenzie King as its Deputy Minister. Molson's continued to own the building during the tenancy of the Department of Labour (1903-1912), and then sold the building to the Bank of Montreal in 1925. Various societies and commercial enterprises occupied the building subsequently, and it is now owned by the National Capital Commission. Extensive renovations over the years have completely altered the character of the interior.

14 Metcalfe Street is a four storey commercial building of red brick accented with contrasting white brick and pale stone. It has an ambitious display of Italianate features, such as wide voussoirs, prominent keystones, voussoir stones that alternate in colour and texture, highly decorative stringcourses, and a prominent, complexly designed cornice. The sculptural details in the voussoirs and in the pilasters are worth examining in some detail.

12

Scottish Ontario Chambers

42-50 Sparks Street
1883

Most people who visit Confederation Square do so to see the War Memorial, which is the centrepiece of this area. While you are here, turn and examine the buildings that encircle the Memorial. Oldest is the East Block (1859-65) of the Parliament Buildings. In front of that is the Parliamentary Fence (1872-74). Going clockwise, next is the Chateau Laurier (1908-12), then the former Union Station (1909-12; now the Government Conference Centre). Beside the canal is the National Arts Centre (1964-69). Across the street on the corner of Queen and Elgin is Central Chambers (1890-91); beside that is the former Bell Block (1867); and then, on the corner of Sparks Street, is the Scottish Ontario Chambers. Across Sparks Street is the Central Post Office (1938-40). This takes us back to Wellington Street and the Langevin Block (1883-89). The range of architectural styles spans more than a century of Canadian architecture, and speaks well of design in this country at almost any point in that time.

The three buildings between Queen and Sparks are

Sparks Street looking west, 1898. Scottish Ontario Chambers at the left.
(National Archives, C 3776)

fine examples of late nineteenth century commercial architecture. The Scottish Ontario Chambers illustrates how well suited the Italianate style was to commercial design. The style was a revival of Renaissance Italian civic and domestic architecture, in particular the urban palaces (or palazzos) of Florence, Venice and Rome. In this building, the compact form of the urban palazzo occupies every square inch of an irregular lot. The segmentally arched openings provide excellent display window space on the ground floor, and well-lit interiors for the offices above. The contrasting tones of brickwork express the Victorian love of colour. This building has housed commercial enterprises throughout its history. It was designed by architect William Hodgson, who built the Bell Block next door.

The presence on Confederation Square of this building, the Bell Block and Central Chambers, is the result of town planning projects of the twentieth century. In the nineteenth century, the land between the Langevin Block and Sussex Drive was a maze of narrow streets dominated by mediocre commercial and industrial buildings. These three buildings were considered the only well designed structures in the area. Appalled by the shabbiness of the city, Prime Minister Sir Wilfrid Laurier formed a commission to study the problem of creating a handsome capital city out of this narrow, dirty industrial town. The Ottawa Improvement Commission and other federal commissions that followed noted the lack of a useful ceremonial space — other than Parliament Hill itself — and recommended the clearing of the land from the Langevin Block to the Canal, in order to create a space for ceremonial activities. The three commercial buildings on the west side of Confederation Square were the only commercial structures that survived these urban renewal projects of the early twentieth century. The character of Confederation Square took its final form in 1939 when King George VI unveiled the War Memorial in honour of those who fell in the First World War.

13

Central Chambers

Elgin and Queen Streets
1890-91

Central Chambers was built as a speculative enterprise by Edward Seybold and James Gibson, dry goods merchants, in what had become Ottawa's principal commercial district. Throughout its history, this building has housed shops on the ground floor and shops and offices above. One of Ottawa's first electric elevators was installed here. Central Chambers has become even more visible since the buildings that once stood on Confederation Square were cleared away to make room for the War Memorial.

Central Chambers in 1898.
(National Archives)

Central Chambers is one of the finest examples of late nineteenth century architecture in the country. Until the 1890s, commercial design had been dominated by the Italianate style, as exemplified by the Scottish Ontario Chambers (see Number 12). But with its regularly spaced and not particularly large windows, the Italianate style was not always satisfactory. Tenants of upper storeys wanted to maximize the light in their work areas, and merchants situated on upper floors wanted their wares visible from the street. In 1871-73, British architect Richard Norman Shaw constructed a commercial building in London, England, called New Zealand Chambers, that was a departure from conventional commercial design. New Zealand Chambers was the first commercial structure to use vertically grouped bay windows — hitherto solely a feature of domestic architecture. Central Chambers was an early imitator in Canada, and it is a successful design indeed. Here the bay windows run vertically through three storeys, and each line of bays is capped by a palladian window and a pointed gable. Stonework on the ground floor piers gives a sense of weight and stability to what is otherwise a very open and airy design. Notice the beautiful architectural details on the building, especially the terra cotta decorative panels, and the decorative carving around the main door.

The architect of Central Chambers was John James Browne, son of architect George Browne. Born in 1837 in Montreal, and educated at the Montreal High School, Browne began practice at the age of nineteen. His works include warehouses, factories, commercial buildings, churches and some residences. He died in 1893, just two years after completing this building.

541 Sussex Drive

541 Sussex Drive
1863

Sussex Drive (or Street as it was originally called) was once lined on both sides with mid-nineteenth century commercial buildings such as this. As Ottawa's prosperity grew and its standing as the new national capital became assured, the wooden shacks of the early century were replaced by these more substantial and quite handsome commercial buildings. Commercial development took place at this time on Rideau Street and on Bank Street as well, but the Sussex buildings are the best preserved. Over the years, this building has seen many tenants come and go. 541 has been home to the British and the Clarendon Hotels. It has been a barracks, an art gallery, and the home of the Geological Survey. In 1961 the National Capital Commission began a programme of rehabilitation for Sussex Street, with the intention of creating an attractive ceremonial route between

Parliament Hill and Government House and 24 Sussex. The successful rehabilitation of these structures has encouraged others to renovate in the Byward Market area, which in turn has spurred economic development here. An attractive courtyard has been created behind these structures.

This building marks the earliest known appearance in Ottawa of the Italianate style, which we have examined already in some Centretown buildings. Here we see many characteristic features of the style: regularly spaced openings, segmental openings over the windows with prominent keystones, a stringcourse, and a heavy cornice overall. All of these features are executed in the grey Ottawa Valley limestone that was most commonly used up to mid-century.

541 Sussex Drive, ca. 1881-1910.
(National Archives)

15

Martineau Hotel

47-61 Murray Street
1872

While this building is now a handsomely renovated structure, it has had a rough history and was not always so respectable. The Martineau Hotel started its existence as a better class hotel, built in 1872 for its original owner, Eugene Martineau, one-time mayor of Ottawa. The hotel changed hands several times, and with the declining fortunes of the Byward Market in the first half of the twentieth century, the hotel declined also, into a flophouse and brothel. But all that has now changed.

In 1977 the Heritage Canada Foundation purchased this building when it was at its most decrepit. With federal and municipal assistance, Heritage Canada restored the shell of the Martineau Hotel as a model of building recycling. A new addition at the back has been sensitively integrated with the older portion on Murray Street. It now houses offices and shops.

European and North American architecture of the eighteenth and early nineteenth centuries was dominated by the principles of classicism, that is, symmetrical buildings with relatively horizontal proportions, evenly spaced openings, and decorative features taken from classical architecture. In high style buildings and in vernacular structures alike, this style held sway for a remarkably long period of time. This building illustrates well the persistence of vernacular classicism well into the second half of the nineteenth century. One can understand the reason for its continuing popularity: the regularity of classicism made it easy and relatively inexpensive to design and erect a simple, utilitarian structure such as this one. The round-arched openings were carriageways leading to the stableyard at the rear.

16

Notre-Dame Basilica

375 Sussex Drive
1841-53

Notre-Dame Basilica.
(National Archives)

On October 25th 1841, the cornerstone was laid for the first stone church to serve the Catholic (largely French and Irish) community of Bytown. The design as originally conceived by the architect, Father John Cannon, was to be entirely classical. Cannon's building rose majestically amid the small shacks of Lowertown, to just above the first storey. Then in 1844 Cannon left the project and Father Pierre-Adrien Telmon took his place.

Telmon's vision of the church that was to arise amid the shacks of Bytown was quite different from Cannon's; it was more ambitious, as suited the changing circumstances. In 1847 the Diocese of Ottawa was created and this building was named the cathedral. A few alterations and enlargements had to be made to accommodate the structure to its new role as the Bishop's seat. Originally the Cathedral was dedicated to the Immaculate Conception. It was renamed Notre-Dame in 1860 and then in 1879 it was raised to the rank of a minor basilica.

With its new status, Notre-Dame became the centre of Ottawa's thriving Catholic community. A Bishop's Palace was begun nearby, as well as the Collège de Bytown, also associated with the Catholic Church, and the convent of the Grey Nuns (Soeurs Grises). The cathedral was opened and consecrated in 1853, but construction continued for many years afterwards. The spires were added in 1858. A polygonal apse was added in 1862. The Madonna and Child between the spires, the work of Spanish sculptor Cordona, was unveiled in 1866.

Notre-Dame Basilica has an oratory plan; that is, it is a long, relatively wide structure with a nave and side aisles ideally laid out for hearing the service and for viewing the Sanctuary.

Telmon was an Oblate father from France and he brought with him the latest taste for the new style: the Gothic Revival. This was a style that used the features of late twelfth to early fifteenth century European architecture, most notably the pointed arch. The Gothic Revival was enthusiastically seized upon by Catholics and Protestants alike, as a symbol of the renewal of Christian faith. One suspects that Telmon longed to tear down all of the existing walls, but such an expense could not be justified. The best he could do was even the walls off, thereby leaving the classical doors of the main facade. Above are pointed windows with the delicate mouldings and tracery of thirteenth century French Gothic architecture. The Gothic Revival theme continues inside, where wonderful sculpture, painting and gilding ornament this superb structure. Flavien Rochon, Philippe Parizeau and Louis-Phillippe Hebert were principally responsible for the carving.

Notre-Dame is the oldest surviving church in Ottawa, and it has been designated under the Ontario Heritage Act.

17

Archbishop's Palace

143 St. Patrick Street
1849-50

When Bishop Guigues was consecrated in 1848, he was residing, along with several other priests, in the Donnelly House on Sussex Drive. Plans were already in existence for a Bishop's Palace to be built to the east of the Basilica, but they had had to be put off as the Basilica was enlarged and the costs of its construction grew. Finally work was begun under the direction, it is thought, of Father Dandurand, who was an architect. His plans were for a large structure to contain offices, reception rooms, dormitories and the Bishop's private suite. Work began in May of 1849 on property first rented and later purchased from the Ordnance Department; exactly one year later, Guigues moved in.

Dandurand's building was remarkable for its time and place. Atop the two storey stone structure is a mansard roof, added probably in 1863, one of the earliest known examples of this type of roof in nineteenth century Canada. The mansard roof was commonly used in French architecture throughout the seventeeth, eighteenth, and nineteenth centuries; the palace of the Louvre is probably the best known example. The mansard, named for architect Louis Mansart, was an economical way of providing for an extra storey of space. It also gave an imposing appearance to the top of any building. The mansard became popular in Canada in the 1870s and 1880s with the appearance of the Second Empire style. The use of the mansard here presages the new style to come, and can be attributed to Dandurand's French origin.

Considerable taste was displayed in the design of this structure. Note the fine architectural details around the main door, the two bay windows, and in the unusual gable dormers that break the roofline. Elsewhere the limestone construction is typical of Ottawa Valley masonry.

In 1888, His Excellency Joseph Thomas Duhamel became the first Archbishop of Ottawa, and so the building has been called the Archbishop's Palace ever since.

Over the years numerous additions were made to the exterior and extensive changes made inside. In the 1970s plans were made to demolish the building; fortunately, it was restored instead by the National Capital Commission and the Ontario Heritage Foundation.

The Most Reverend Eugene Guigues, 1865.
(National Archives)

Valade House

142 St. Patrick Street
ca. 1865

This delightful house was architecturally a cut above the more typical Lowertown house, which one can see at Rochon House, 138 St. Patrick, next door. Notice the fine carving around the front entrance, the large windows and the gracious second floor balcony. The Valade house signals the attractive mix of English and French influences characteristic of much Ottawa Valley architecture. The regularity of the facade and the classical details around the door derive from the eighteenth and early nineteenth century classicism that the British brought to this country. It harmonized well with the steep roofs, prominent dormers, balconies and casement windows of Quebec architecture. Such balconies were to become a much more common sight in French Canadian urban domestic structures, especially in Montreal. A balcony such as this would give a family a pleasant place to sit outside in the hot summer weather. Most backyards in the nineteenth century were entirely given over to utilitarian purposes: laundry, privy, well and, for a wealthy family, a stable and carriage house.

Most doctors in the nineteenth century had their offices in their own homes, and this house was no exception. Dr. Francois-Xavier Valade moved into this house in 1866 and remained here until his death in 1918. His office was on the ground floor and his pharmacy in the storey above. Valade had an interesting brush with history: he was one of the doctors who examined the Metis leader Louis Riel in 1885 to determine his sanity before his trial. The Valade family connection to the Northwest spanned the generations. Valade's daughter married Joseph Royal, who was later Lieutenant Governor of the Northwest Territories from 1888 to 1893.

The Rochon house next door dates from 1832, and is a rare surviving example of working class housing of the era.

The Valade house was purchased by the National Capital Commission in 1967.

19

La Salle Academy

373 Sussex Drive
1852

At the time of its construction, the La Salle Academy (originally called the Collège de Bytown) was one of the grandest buildings in eastern Ontario. It rose an imposing three storeys; as originally designed, it had two projecting end pieces of two bays each, with a centre section set back (farther than it is now) leading up to a handsome pediment. The fundamental classicism of this design grew out of eighteenth century design, in particular the work of British architects inspired by the Italian designer, Andrea Palladio. British architects designed buildings in which a centre section was flanked by side pavilions, wings or projections. This tripartite formula was used for houses and public buildings in Great Britain and in the colonies alike. Such structures were usually built of stone, as here, and handsomely finished off with finely carved corner quoins, keystones and other detail work.

The Academy was, at the time of its construction, one of the most progressive institutions in Upper Canada. It was begun by the Oblate order, which concerned itself to a great extent with educational matters. When the Oblates arrived in Bytown in 1844, there was no educational system to speak of. Teachers were independent entrepreneurs, who provided their own classrooms and their own fuel for winter. Bishop Guigues quickly made plans to correct this appalling situation. At first he had a school opened up in a small wooden structure. Then this fine building was opened up in 1852 as the College de Bytown, a bilingual institution open to Catholics and Protestants, rich and poor alike. This was Ottawa's first major school, and its imposing architecture was a clear statement of the value placed on education by the Oblate order.

So successful was the College that it outgrew the building and had to move to a larger structure in nearby Sandy Hill; this latter institution became the University of Ottawa. The Church retained ownership of the Sussex Street building, renting it out as a first class hotel. It was commandeered briefly in the 1860s as a military barracks, and once the troops left in 1870 it became a school again. This time the Congregation of Christian Brothers moved in and set up Notre-Dame School. The school was renamed La Salle School in 1888 in honour of the founder of the Christian Brothers, Jean Baptiste de La Salle. Cramped for space, the Brothers filled in the recess between the two projections and put on the present mansard roof. This building remained a centre for education until 1971 when the Ecole Secondaire de La Salle (as it was now known) moved elsewhere.

The building was purchased in 1971 by the Ministry of State for Urban Affairs, which renovated it as a showcase of urban renewal. Unfortunately all that remains of the original structure are the exterior masonry walls. Virtually nothing survived a century of alterations, and so the present interior is entirely modern.

20

Donnelly House

365 Sussex Drive
1844

The Donnelly House belongs to the school of British classicism that dominated early nineteenth century design in Ottawa. This is clearly shown in its handsome yet sober design with its strict, bilateral symmetry, centre door and moderately pitched roof. Note the graceful adamesque fanlight over the door. This was very much an urban structure. If you look at the gable ends you will notice that the side walls rise slightly higher than the roofline. The timberwork of roof structures was often the villain in the spread of many urban fires, and so fire walls such as this were commonly constructed in areas where structures were built close together. The Donnelly house was built very close to the thoroughfare (albeit not as close as it is now, as a result of the widening of Sussex Drive) in the manner of European urban residences. This was the middle of Bytown, a bustling community whose close-packed nature is still evident.

The history of the Donnelly House reflects the history of the Irish and French community in Lowertown. During the building of the canal and for many years afterwards, Lowertown was the home of many of the Irish and French labourers associated with the canal and with the timber trade. This house was built by an Irishman named Thomas Donnelly, who lived here until 1847. During these years, the Collège de Bytown and Notre-Dame Church (later the Basilica) were under construction, and the new Bishop of Ottawa needed a residence. Bishop Joseph-Eugène Bruno Guigues rented the Donnelly House from 1847 to 1850 until his own residence around the corner on St. Patrick was completed. After that the house reverted to a private dwelling for the remainder of the nineteenth century. In 1899 the Roman Catholic church bought the house and it was part of the Cathedral complex for nearly all of this century. In 1971 the federal government purchased this building and renovated it.

21

Rathier House

193 Cumberland
ca. 1862

Lowertown in about 1911.
(National Archives C 6547)

This house sits on land that was originally part of the property of the Board of Ordnance. In 1823, Lord Dalhousie, Governor of British North America, purchased tracts of land on either side of the future canal site in order to secure territory for the project. Three years later, Lieutenant-Colonel By designated this a townsite and had it surveyed for lots. He specified that the lots be leased for thirty years from the Board of Ordnance rather than purchased, in order to discourage speculation. It appears that a wooden building stood on this site until 1862, when a carpenter named Abraham Rathier erected this combination house and grocery store for himself.

Although built in the second half of the nineteenth century, this house/store is more like commercial premises of the first half. During the early part of the century, structures erected for commercial purposes were hardly distinguishable from houses. This is not surprising since merchants tended still to live above their place of business. Later, more affluent merchants would live in a fashionable residential part of town and erect a structure in the commercial district that was strictly for business. For the small entrepreneur, however, the combination of house and store remained a satisfactory arrangement. Here, this two and a half storey stone structure with evenly spaced windows looks very much like other houses of the era, with the exception of the corner door on the ground floor.

This house/store passed through very many hands over the years, and well into this century it still had a store on the ground floor. Now it is solely residential, but it still fits in with the atmosphere of a bustling market district.

22

Earnscliffe

Sussex Drive
1857

Earnscliffe is a fine example of a Gothic Revival country villa. The most characteristic feature of the style seen here is the label moulding around the windows, characteristic of secular medieval building. The pointed arch of Gothic architecture more properly belonged on ecclesiastical buildings, and was considered unsuitable for domestic building. Country villas were often large, architecturally ambitious structures. Architects looked to the country parsonages of the later middle ages as good models to follow for composition and detailing. These were large, rambling, asymmetrical residences, with steep roofs, prominent gables, roughcast stone or half-timbering, casement windows, oak carving, and so forth. Such features corresponded well with the nineteenth century taste for picturesque design. The results were houses such as Earnscliffe, a sizeable house with a steep roof, jutting gables, dormer windows, projections that create effects of light and shade, bargeboards that stand in silhouette against the shadows that they cast, and attractive windows from which to admire the view.

The best view of this house is from the Macdonald-Cartier Bridge. From here one can appreciate the breathtaking setting of the house, perched on the edge of a steep decline into the Ottawa River. At one time the river would have been a busy sight: timber rafts on their way to Britain, log booms headed for the pulp and paper mills, steamships running back and forth from Montreal. Logs still descend the Gatineau River, opposite, but most of the traffic on the river now is pleasure craft.

Earnscliffe was built for John MacKinnon, a son-in-law and business partner of Thomas MacKay, the builder of the mills at the Rideau Falls and the developer of New Edinburgh. The house was later acquired by another relative of MacKay's, Thomas Coltrin Keefer. The most distinguished resident of this house, however, was Sir John A. Macdonald, first Prime Minister of

Earnscliffe in 1891.
(National Archives)

Sir John A. Macdonald, in 1890.
(National Archives, C 686)

Canada. Macdonald rented the house in 1870-71 and again in 1882. He finally purchased it in 1883 and remained here until his death in 1891. The house was bequeathed to Macdonald's widow, but in 1900 Lady Macdonald sold the house and went to Scotland for the remainder of her life. The house was acquired by the Government of the United Kingdom as a residence for the High Commissioner. The British government has maintained the house and grounds well.

Earnscliffe is a National Historic Site.

23

Fraser School House

62-64 John Street
1837

The original village of New Edinburgh was founded by Thomas MacKay. Born in Scotland, MacKay was a stone mason by trade and an entrepreneur by inclination. Upon his arrival in Canada he first worked on the

Lachine Canal. It was here that he gained experience of construction in Canadian conditions, putting him in a good position to become one of the chief contractors on the Rideau Canal. With the money he earned on the Canal, MacKay purchased property at the mouth of the Rideau River. He harnessed the power of the falls for a saw mill, a grist mill, a woollen mill and a distillery. MacKay laid out residential lots nearby for his employees and named the settlement after his native city in Scotland. New Edinburgh became a village in 1867 and was incorporated into the city of Ottawa some twenty years later.

MacKay built this structure in 1837 as workers' housing. It is thought that one year later he made the building available to the village as a school, with the classroom on one side and the schoolmaster, James Fraser, living in the other. About 1843 it reverted to domestic use and remained working class housing until purchased by the National Capital Commission in 1959. Originally the National Capital Commission had intended to rip down all the structures on this city block, feeling that their working class character was out of step with the nearby French Embassy and the Prime

Minister's residence. Out of respect for the age of this building and its close association with the community of New Edinburgh, the National Capital Commission spared the building and restored it.

Fraser School House before renovation.
(City of Ottawa Archives)

Built of rubble stone, symmetrical, capped with a gable roof and having paired end chimneys, this is a modest yet dignified structure. The building has undergone a number of changes over the years. During the restoration conducted by the National Capital Commission in 1967 the dormers were removed because they were thought not to date from the original date of construction. A wood shingle roof was applied and the interior walls were removed. More drastic than the changes to the building have been the changes to the environment. New Edinburgh is no longer an industrial centre; the mills that once lined the river are long gone, and the neighbourhood — once modest and working class — has been thoroughly gentrified. The school house once sat amid other structures like itself, but it now stands quite alone. Now the school house is occupied by Heritage Ottawa, which uses it for offices and display space.

MacKay's Mills at the Rideau Falls.
(National Archives, pa 51837)

24

Henderson House

34 Alexander
1860-62

The Second Empire style was originally intended for monumental, public structures, such as the Langevin Block (see Number 5). When its characteristic mansard roof was adapted to a smaller building, the effect could be almost comical. No doubt the architect of the John Henderson house had fun with this design: the roof looks like an oversized hat pulled down low over the wearer's ears and eyes. All the details are nicely done; notice the mouldings along the eaves and around the windows.

In the nineteenth century, woodworking reached a level of creative excellence that has not been reached since. Canada's rich timber reserves were put to artistic use in structures large and small, aided by the development of sophisticated mechanical saws. Each historical revival style had its repertoire of decorative details that builders translated into wooden ornament. There were paired brackets for the Italianate, finials and crockets for the Gothic Revival, and dentils and triglyphs for the classical styles. Here, woodwork has been used to ornament the mansard roof of the Second Empire style. While far from the formality of the monumental European buildings which inspired the Second Empire style, this house is a fresh, inventive creation indicative of a genuine folk art.

The Henderson House was originally the home of John Henderson, manager of the Maclaren Lumber company, and one-time City Clerk.

25

35 MacKay/71 Thomas

35 MacKay / 71 Thomas
ca. 1864-65

35 MacKay/71 Thomas was once a single family dwelling. With its centre door, window to either side and moderately pitched roof, it is a type of house commonly found in Eastern Ontario, although a rare survivor in the city of Ottawa. The house is a simple design, yet it is an excellent illustration of the beauty that can be achieved by simple means. The nicely judged proportions, and the contrast of rough stone walls with smooth corner quoins is very satisfying. It has been suggested that the house was built by Thomas MacKay to accommodate some of the workers in his nearby mills along the Rideau River. Sometime in the 1870s the house was subdivided into two residences and it has remained so ever since.

In the 1920s architect Allan Keefer added the delicate, columned porches that we see today, and they are in keeping with the original design of the house. This was not an unusual thing to do. We tend to think of the heritage movement as a movement that appeared in reaction to the widespread destruction of our architectural heritage that took place in the 1960s and 1970s. But there was an earlier heritage movement in this century, that took place in the 1920s and 30s. At this time, modern architects were designing structures modelled after the colonial architecture of the eighteenth and early nineteenth centuries. In English Canada, so called 'Georgian' houses were popular, while in Quebec the 'maison traditionelle' was all the rage. It was natural that, in designing new structures on an old theme, architects came to appreciate and respect historic architecture. Many historical societies came into existence at this time, and considerable work was done to save many important sites, including several fortresses that are now national historic sites. Historic buildings that were "modernized" in the 1920s and 1930s were often given a very sympathetic treatment, as we see here in Keefer's delicate porches.

26

7 Rideau Gate

7 Rideau Gate
1861-62

Industrialist Henry Osgoode Burritt, owner of the Rideau Falls Milling Company, had this house built for himself in 1861-62. In 1884 the house was acquired by the eighth Earl of Cavan for the use of his son, the Honourable Octavius Lambert. The Lambert family resided here for many years. Commodore P.W. Nelles purchased the house in 1934 and contracted Toronto architect Mackenzie Waters to work on it. Waters removed the verandah and built a garage with sleeping quarters attached, and gave the exterior the Georgian Revival treatment that it has today. In 1947 Nelles sold the house to Thomas Ahearn, an Ottawa businessman. He commissioned the Ottawa firm of Hazelgrove, Lithwick and Cameron to build a sunroom and a two storey addition. The federal government acquired the house in 1966 and refurbished it as an

7 Rideau Gate.
(National Archives)

official guest house. It opened in time for the Centennial celebrations in 1967. The federal government made no significant exterior changes, but the interior has been upgraded significantly to suit it to its official role.

This house was one of a number of villas constructed at the same time in what was then becoming Ottawa's elite suburb. Nearby are 5 Rideau Gate, Earnscliffe, MacKay's mansion (now Rideau Hall), 24 Sussex (now the home of the Prime Minister), as well as other fine residences that have since disappeared. At this time a move to picturesque, rural retreats, away from the noise, open sewers and foul air of the city core was taking place in cities throughout Canada. The owners could enjoy the quality of life in the country while being only a short carriage ride away from their place of work.

As the official guest residence of the Government of Canada, 7 Rideau Gate is much altered from its original appearance. There used to be a wide verandah across the front and down one side. The eaves were once deep and ornamented with scrolls, and there was once a widow's walk atop the truncated hip roof. While these elements are gone, one can still appreciate the quality of the stonework, witness to the craftsmanship of the masons of the Ottawa Valley.

7 Rideau Gate is part of an enclave of official residences. It is at the end of the ceremonial route that begins at Parliament Hill and terminates at 24 Sussex and Rideau Hall. Nearby also are the embassies of South Africa and France.

27

Embassy of South Africa

5 Rideau Gate
circa 1841

When this house was built, it was one of only a very few stone houses in New Edinburgh, the other principal one being MacKay's Mansion (now Rideau Hall). 5 Rideau Gate appears to have been only one or one and a half storeys high originally, but from the beginning it had the classical symmetry that one would expect of houses of this era. 5 Rideau Gate has been extensively remodelled over the years. Many of the interior mouldings appear to date from the 1870s; they are large and rounded and quite unlike the flattish, delicate mouldings of the 1840s. In 1920, prominent Ottawa architect W.E. Noffke (who designed the Embassy of the Union of Soviet Socialist Republics on Charlotte Street) was engaged to make some alterations and additions. His work was so thorough that one might consider this house as good an example of taste in the early twentieth century as in the early nineteenth.

The first inhabitant of the house was James Stevenson, manager of the Bank of Montreal in Bytown. Then, in 1867, the house passed to Moss K. Dickinson, mayor of Ottawa. Other prominent citizens lived here until 1944 when it was purchased by the government of South Africa.

28

Rideau Hall Gatehouse

13A Sussex Drive
1868

Thomas MacKay.
(National Archives)

In 1857 an architectural competition was held at the same time as the competition for the Parliament Buildings, for the design of a viceregal mansion to be situated on Nepean Point, roughly where the National Gallery is today. Although a design was chosen, the mansion was not built because the costs of the Parliament Buildings had escalated so severely. Looking around for temporary accommodation for the Governor General, the government found that there was only one house that was suitable for the Queen's representative: MacKay's Castle in New Edinburgh. Thomas MacKay was a stonemason who had made his fortune contracting on the Rideau Canal, and on the mills that he owned along the Rideau River. MacKay had built himself a lovely regency house, nicknamed MacKay's Castle, in the midst of an 80 acre site. In 1865 the government rented MacKay's Castle and made several additions which substantially enlarged it. Viscount Monck, the first Governor General, made improvements to the grounds as well. He had the present fence and gatehouse constructed, to designs of architect F.P. Rubidge of the Department of Public Works. It cost $950.00 to build and it was finished in 1868. In 1869 the government purchased the entire estate from MacKay and this has been the residence of the Governor General ever since.

Additions and alterations to the main house have been so extensive that it is more a building of the twentieth century than the nineteenth. This is why the main building does not appear in this book.

A sizeable estate such as this needed a number of service buildings. This estate had an ice house, laundry, stables, carriage house, staff quarters, gas plant and, of course, a gatehouse. Since the landscaping of a large estate was an important consideration, these ancillary structures had to be attractive as well as functional. Certainly the gatehouse makes a very good first impression upon those entering the grounds. Its octagonal plan is quite unusual. The architectural features are from the Italianate style; notice the prominent horizontal channelling in the stonework, and the wide voussoirs over the windows. The carved heads in the keystones of the arches are particularly characteristic of the Italianate style, as we saw before in discussing Canada's Four Corners (Number 10).

In 1938 an addition and alterations were made to the gatehouse. The interior was subdivided to create a washroom, kitchen, pantry and dining room.

29

St. Bartholemew's Anglican Church

125 MacKay Street
1868

In the early nineteenth century, there arose a reform movement within the Anglican Church which was to be tremendously influential in the evolution of church architecture for the rest of the century. This movement called for a return to the liturgy and the architecture of the Church as it had been in medieval times, before the Reformation. The classical design of churches of the eighteenth century was abandoned in favour of churches that were very close in design to medieval parish churches. Such a church is St. Bartholemew's. Like St. Alban the Martyr in Sandy Hill (Number 37), it imitates a medieval English parish church. It has the steep, massive roof, low rough stone walls and heavy piers of the medieval model. St. Bartholemew's has a more decorative quality to it, and is less stern in design than St. Alban's. The decorative carving around the doors, dormers and the park-like setting of St. Bartholemew's soften its appearance.

The parish of St. Bartholemew's includes Rideau Hall, and so this church has been the place of worship of many of our governors general. Many mementos inside are their gifts to the church. A modern addition to one side harmonizes well with the old church.

New Edinburgh has managed to retain its village atmosphere, perhaps more successfully than other older Ottawa neighbourhoods. St. Bartholemew's contributes significantly to the sense of a small, comfortable community.

The architect of St. Bartholemew's was Canada's first dominion Chief Architect from 1872 to 1881. Thomas S. Scott (1836-1895) was born in Birkenhead, England, and studied architecture under his brother Walter. Scott arrived in Canada in 1863 and was in private practice until his appointment as Chief Architect began. The Old Toronto Union Station and the Old Bonaventure Station in Montreal were both done while he was in private practice. As head of the Department of Public Works, Scott guided the design of federal buildings all across the new dominion.

30

W.R. Latchie House

25-29 Chrichton Street
ca. 1868

The Latchie house was built to house mill workers from the nearby mills along the Rideau River. It is a well designed double, and one might easily mistake it for a single family dwelling.

Until the mid-nineteenth century, wooden construction was less favoured than stone or brick construction. If one had the money, one built in these more permanent materials. The prejudice against wood began to change slowly, as certain architects and writers worked to change public opinion. They pointed out that wood was the most common building material in North America, that people on this continent were particularly skilled at woodworking, and that it was time, perhaps, to make a virtue of necessity. Writers like American Andrew Jackson Downing published books of plans for buildings that suggested the artistic possibilities of wood. One of the least expensive ways to ornament a small building was the application of board and batten siding.

Board and batten sheathing enjoyed a measure of popularity in the second half of the nineteenth century. Boards were nailed vertically over the frame, with sides abutting each other, and a narrow strip (or batten) of wood was nailed over the joint. As a facing material it was relatively inexpensive and easy to install, while providing a modest building with a great deal of visual interest.

31

92 Stanley Avenue

92 Stanley Avenue
ca. 1867

A charming and unpretentious house, 92 Stanley Avenue was the home of J. Dougal MacLeod. MacLeod, a native of the Isle of Skye, Scotland, was a miller in the employ of Thomas MacKay. MacKay sold the land to MacLeod in 1867, and the house was probably built soon after.

In its thick, stone walls, and its air of quiet dignity, the house suggests its origins in the architecture of distant Scotland. Like many New Edinburgh houses, 92 Stanley sits close to the street. Although New Edinburgh has lost its industrial buildings and its houses have been gentrified, one can still perceive that it was once a working class neighbourhood. 92 Stanley Avenue has changed hands many times over the years and has recently been restored.

Hundreds of smaller stone houses of this size were built in eastern Ontario in the early nineteenth century. Most were symmetrical, having a centre door flanked by one to two windows on either side; a few were picturesque, asymmetrical designs such as this one. Typically these houses have a gently pitched gable roof, widely spaced, sash windows, and little in the way of decorative detail. What decoration existed was usually executed in wood and concentrated around the door. Generally these houses sit on thick, rubble fieldstone foundations, with broad wooden beams supporting the floors and roof. Chimneys are placed in the gable ends. The walls of stone houses are necessarily thick, making for deep window sills inside. Interior finish was usually plaster over lath or, less commonly, plaster directly on the stone.

32

Minto Bridges

New Edinburgh to Green Island
1900

A city intersected by many waterways, Ottawa has required good bridges from its first settlement days. The first bridge linked Ottawa and Hull across the Chaudière Falls (1826-28), and was the work of engineer Lieutenant Colonel John By. By and the Corps of Royal Engineers also built the original Sappers' Bridge over the eight locks of the Rideau Canal. Other bridges followed and

The Minto Bridges in the 1920s.
(National Archives, PA 34274)

several are worth a visit, including the Pretoria Bridge (1978-81, a reconstruction of the 1915-17 bridge), the Chaudière Bridge (1914), and the Interprovincial Bridge (1900).

A straightforward cantilevered design with a minimum of decorative crestwork, the Minto Bridges integrate well with their pastoral setting. These bridges were once the principal link between Rideau Hall and the Parliament Buildings, and they were named for the fourth Earl of Minto, who was Governor General at the time that these bridges were constructed. The bridges were the work of the Dominion Bridge Company of Montreal, which was one of the principal contractors in the country for steel frame construction of both bridges and buildings.

The engineer of the Minto Bridges was Robert Surtees. Surtees was born in Yorkshire, England in 1835, and apprenticed there as an engineer. He arrived in Canada at age 21, and first lived in Hamilton, where he was the Assistant City Engineer. Surtees later moved to Ottawa, where he became City Engineer. He worked on various drainage and sewage projects, and designed the Carleton County Court House (Number 33) and the Ottawa Protestant Hospital. He died in 1906.

33, 34 and 35

Former Carleton County Court House

Former City Registry Office

Former Carleton County Jail

Nicholas Street

The administration of justice was a serious matter in nineteenth century Canada, and dotted across our land are solid, imperturbable buildings which attest to the importance of the rule of law, even in an emerging frontier society. In 1841 Bytown councillors voted to build a court house on land donated by the lumber magnate Nicholas Sparks. The first building lasted many years, until it was destroyed by fire in 1870. In this earlier modest court house Patrick James Whelan stood trial for the assassination of Thomas D'Arcy McGee, one of Canada's leading politicians and a Father of Confederation. Found guilty of murder, Whelan was hanged in the court yard of the jail on February 11, 1869, in Canada's last public execution.

Carleton County Court House
(City of Ottawa Archives)

City Registry Office, 1954.
(City of Ottawa Archives)

In 1870-71 a new court house was constructed, larger and more imposing than the modest original. City Engineer Robert Surtees designed the court house to blend in with the Carleton County Jail, which had been constructed in 1860-62 by H.H. Horsey. Two Registry offices were built nearby. The County of Carleton Registry Office, a stone structure meant to match the Court House and Jail, was constructed in 1870-71. The City of Ottawa Registry Office, a brick and stone structure built in 1873, is illustrated here.

These buildings form a remarkable grouping of civic design in the second half of the nineteenth century. The landscaping and fencing were designed to integrate them into a large and imposing complex of inter-related buildings.

The three buildings illustrated here are all in the Italianate style, which was used principally on commercial structures. It was considered appropriate for civic buildings for its handsome and dignified appearance, and for its reference to the rise of civic government in Renaissance Italy. Although these buildings are in the

Gallows of Carleton County Jail.
(City of Ottawa Archives)

same style, they are all quite different interpretations. The largest of the three, the court house, uses rusticated stone for the wall surface, contrasted by smoothly finished stone for the stringcourses, quoins and window mouldings. Similar but much smaller is the registry office across the street, a brick interpretation of the same style. Here oversized stone mouldings of alternating thicknesses ornament the openings, and give this tiny building a rather gargantuan aspect. Yet a third interpretation of the Italianate style is the Jail next to the court house. Here the architectural details are similar, the round-headed windows with prominent lintels, and the contrastic textures of stone. Yet the effect is quite different: it is stern and unfriendly, an appropriate treatment for a jail.

Despite the grim appearance of the jail, it was considered a model institution in its day, and was the result of years of study on the part of penal reformers. Here, prisoners were to be separated by types and severity of crime, and by their ages, and their behaviour was to be changed by work, isolation, proper diet and exercise. To this end, this building included larger windows, better sanitation and kitchen facilities, an exercise yard and larger cells.

Altogether, this group made an impressive statement of the establishment of civil authority in Ottawa. Today the old court house is used for a gallery and meetings, while the jail houses a different kind of tenant: it is a youth hostel. The gallows remain intact.

36

195 Nicholas Street

195 Nicholas Street
1883-84

This house was built for Horace C. Odell, a brick mason and brickyard owner, as a wedding present for his son, Clarence. Clarence Odell, president of the Ottawa Cord and Tassell Company, lived here until 1903, and after this date the house changed hands many times. It has been used for a doctor's offices and a boarding house. It was acquired by the University of Ottawa in the 1970s and the University painted the building grey and installed false ceilings and partitions throughout. For a while the building stood empty, and was badly damaged by vandals. In 1975 the house was acquired by the National Capital Commission and restored.

Despite its small size, 195 Nicholas Street is a charming example of the Second Empire style. Named for Emperor Louis Napoleon III of France, the Second Empire style appeared in Canada in the late 1860s and remained popular for the following two decades. The style is characterized by a tall mansard roof. Other features of the style are also visible on this building: round-headed dormers, lintels with prominent keystones, and a square tower.

The house retains some of its fine Victorian interior of heavily plastered ceilings and ornate staircase and mantlepieces. The house has a centre hall plan with parlour to one side, dining, kitchen and library on the other. The driveshed at the rear was converted to office space around 1910.

37

St. Alban the Martyr Anglican Church

125 Daly
1867

St. Alban the Martyr was built in response to the growth of the city into the Sandy Hill area. So large had the Anglican congregation become that it could no longer be accommodated in Christ Church on Sparks Street, and a new parish was created in 1865. The architect of the Centre Block and Library of the Parliament Buildings, Thomas Fuller, was called in to design a church for the new congregation. Construction began on the site, but the contractors soon discovered that the land was nothing but shifting sand. A pupil of Fuller's, King Arnoldi, revised the plan, eliminating a tower which the subsoil could not support. The church opened for use in 1867 with the chancel and transept incomplete. These were finished ten years later.

In the 1830s a movement began at Oxford University in England to reform many of the abuses that had become common in the Anglican church. The Trac-

St. Alban's in 1897.
(National Archives)

tarian movement, as it was called, wanted a return to the rites and services of the pre-Reformation church. Many of the ideas advanced by the Tractarians were put into practice, and to reflect these changes it was also thought necessary to design a different kind of church building. The Reformation church was a wide hall with galleries ideally suited for hearing the sermon. But now the sermon was considered less important than the service, and so the galleries were eliminated and the long, narrow hall of the medieval church came into use once again. Architects revived the form of the medieval parish church with its massive, exposed timber roof, low, rustic walls, simple openings, chancel, bellcote, transepts and north porch. The triangular volumes hug the ground and yet reach skywards at the same time. The result is a restrained, thoughtful design that is very pleasing to the eye. With its low, solid stone walls, massive, steep roof, thick buttresses and plain mouldings, St. Alban the Martyr exemplifies the Anglican parish church.

Many of Ottawa's political elite worshipped here, including Sir John A. Macdonald, Sir Francis Hincks, Sir Leonard Tilley, and Sir Charles Tupper. Recently the church has undergone an extensive renovation.

38

Besserer House

149 Daly
1844

The Besserer House was one of the first buildings in the new neighbourhood of Sandy Hill. In 1828, Quebec notary Louis T. Besserer received a grant of land known locally as the Sandy Hill District. Besserer was unable

Besserer House.
(National Archives)

to take up residence on his new property for ten years, since he was sitting as a member of the Legislative Assembly of Lower Canada. He lived elsewhere in Bytown until his own home on Daly Avenue was constructed in 1844. Besserer had his sizable property surveyed for building lots, but it was not until the arrival in the 1860s of the civil service of the newly created federal government that Sandy Hill was settled.

Besserer's house illustrates the persistence of the classically inspired house into the mid-nineteenth century. With its slender casement windows and columned porch, it is a handsome house indeed. The walls are made of roughly shaped stones, framed by finely carved corner quoins. Originally the hipped roof was capped by a widow's walk, which must have afforded a wonderful view of the Ottawa River and the Gatineau Hills. The north facing verandah still survives, although the view is blocked.

The house remained in the Besserer family until 1870; thereafter it passed through many hands. Over the years some changes have been made. A stone veneer kitchen wing was added in 1918, so that the original kitchen and servants' quarters in the basement could be converted to a sitting room and various utility rooms. In the 1960s many of the interior mouldings were replaced.

39

199-205 Daly Avenue

199-205 Daly Avenue
1870s

These modestly designed town houses consist of three units, each with a side hall plan (that is, the door and stairs to one side), two windows to one side of the door, and a height of two and a half storeys. The segmentally arched brick lintels are Italianate in origin. The soft red brick with pale yellow brick trim is modestly done, yet very different from the monochrome stone that we have examined so far. The idea of multicoloured building materials (polychromy), introduced to the Ottawa area by the Parliament Buildings, was beginning to take hold, and to interest builders of even quite modest structures.

By the 1860s and 1870s brick buildings began to appear in Ottawa. In other parts of the country, such as southwestern Ontario, brick had been used as a building material from the earliest days of settlement because of the proximity of large clay beds. But no such clay beds existed in the Ottawa area and so only wood and stone appeared. Thanks to the relative isolation of early settlements, architecture before the mid nineteenth century was strongly rooted in local materials, skills, and the tastes of different ethnic groups. But railways changed all that. Suddenly it was much easier to market materials over a wide geographic area, and clients were quick to accept the greater variety in design that was now possible.

Renovated heritage houses such as these are much sought after. They illustrate how much can be achieved with minimum intervention. The brick has been cleaned, the windows replaced with new windows that approximate the old ones in design, and the new porches are in tune with the style of the houses.

40

Patterson House

336 Daly Avenue
1870

The Patterson house is a fine example of the Victorian Picturesque. The Picturesque was an approach to design rather than an architectural style. It rejected the formality of classical design — symmetrical facades, regularity of openings and so on — in favour of more casual designs, buildings that looked as though they were designed from the inside out, with rooms thrusting off in whatever direction their function dictated. Picturesque design demanded a close relationship between the building and its setting, and the grounds around such houses were carefully planted to set the structure off to best effect, in short, to make the house look like the central element in a picture.

The decorative details of the Patterson house contribute to its picturesque quality. It has contrasting pale yellow brick for window trim of varying widths, for corner quoins, and for a thin stringcourse between the storeys. Notice the attractive design of the sculpted chimney stacks and the elaborately carved bargeboards in the eaves. The asymmetrical composition of the house, the off-centre gable, and the effects of light and shade are all features of picturesque design. Here they combine well with the Victorian love of colour and texture, which was just beginning to appear in architecture.

This house is on property that was originally part of Louis T. Besserer's land grant (see the Besserer House, Number 38). The lot was purchased in the 1860s by a grocer named Thomas Patterson. About 1870 the house was built, and the Pattersons lived in it until 1890, when it was rented out. Lawrence Fennings Taylor, an architect in the firm of Horwood, Taylor and Horwood purchased the house in 1906 and lived here until 1947. Around 1912 he converted the servants' wing in the back into a separate dwelling. Later the main house was subdivided into two residences and has remained a double ever since.

41

Toller House

229 Chapel
1875

The Toller house is typical of larger houses built in the 1870s. Its is a generously sized structure, with a certain angularity to its projections and pointed gables, and relatively small windows. Like many houses of the 1870s, the use of historical revival details is somewhat ambiguous. The voussoirs over the windows are Italianate in origin, and on the upper storey the voussoirs almost come to a Gothic point. The truncated hip roof is Second Empire in inspiration. Originally the house contained a drawing room, library, sitting room, dining room and kitchen on the first floor, five bedrooms on the second floor and two more bedrooms in the attic.

The house was designed by the prominent Ottawa architectural firm of Horsey and Sheard, who had also designed the former Ottawa City Hall (now demolished). The first resident of the house was J.H. Plummer, manager of the Bank of Commerce. Other residents have included Telesphore Fournier, a judge of the Supreme Court, and Frederick Toller, Comptroller of Dominion Currency. The house has had many other tenants, including the Soeurs Missionaires de Notre Dame d'Afrique.

42

Philomene Terrace

363-83 Daly
1874

Among the oldest — and finest — of Ottawa's nine-teenth century row houses is Philomene Terrace. Built in 1874, the row was the work of owner Honore Robillard, a stonemason of considerable repute, and the son of one of the stonemasons who worked on the Rideau Canal. Robillard was a contractor and entre-preneur as well, and served between 1887 and 1896 as a Member of Parliament. He lived for some years in two of these units and rented out the others.

The stonework of Philomene Terrace is beautifully done, and its combination of smooth bands and mould-ings with heavy rustication was typical of masonry work in the second half of the nineteenth century. Smooth bands help organize the facade by delineating the in-dividual storeys and the separate units. In other regards, the design of Philomene Terrace is quite old-fashioned for its time. With its horizontal proportions, low-pitched roofline and evenly spaced openings, it would not have looked out of place on a building erected fifty years previously. The ground floor plan, too, was quite typical of row housing of the early nineteenth century: a side entrance with a staircase and hall, with the parlour and dining room opposite. In the 1890s porches were added to the front, and a kitchen wing added to the back so that the kitchens could be brought up from the basements to the ground floors.

Despite years of neglect, fires and frequent changes of tenancy, the interiors of these houses retained many of their original features. There are marble and wood fireplaces, handsomely carved staircases, and rich plaster mouldings. Thanks to the success of the heritage movement, homes such as these are treasured for their beauty and uniqueness, and their future seems assured.

This terrace has seen many residents come and go, including poet Archibald Lampman. Two of the units were much run down by the 1970s when the City ac-quired them. As an example of what could be done with an older structure, the City renovated the two units of Philomene Terrace and then sold them.

43

464 Besserer

464 Besserer
1873-74

464 Besserer has a delightfully quirky design. Several of its unusual features draw our attention, such as the curious proportions of the large main storey and the squat upper storey. Odd, too, is the mansard roof with its oversized brackets, and the heavily elaborated dormers. The house has an air of preciousness to it, rather like a large Victorian doll's house. The den at the side and the front porch were added later, and were well designed to harmonize with the original structure.

David Ewart.
(National Archives, PA 129119)

Why such a whimsical design? The answer probably lies in the character of the first owner of the house, who was also its designer, architect David Ewart. Ewart was born in 1843 in Scotland, and he was educated there at the Edinburgh School of Art. He came to Canada as a young man; in 1871 he was appointed Assistant Engineer and Architect to the Department of Public Works. Some of his earliest projects included the Canadian Buildings at the Paris Exposition and at the Chicago World's Fair.

In 1897 Ewart became Dominion Chief Architect. From the time of his appointment until his retirement in 1914, Ewart was responsible for a great number of federal buildings erected across the country. Some of his noteworthy structures were the Royal Canadian Mint, the Dominion Archives (now the War Museum), the Connaught Building, the Victoria Memorial Museum (now the National Museum of Natural Sciences), and the Royal Observatory. Ewart was decorated by the French government and invested in the Imperial Service Order in 1903. For most of his career, he was an architect of sombre and imposing structures, serious in design and intent, the stuff of which nations are built. His own house suggests, though, that for all that, the man probably had a sense of humour.

44

Stadacona Hall

395 Laurier Avenue East
ca. 1871

Stadacona Hall in 1891.
(National Archives)

Stadacona Hall has been home to a succession of distinguished families. The house was built in 1871 for lumberman John A. Cameron. Cameron lived here for a while, and then rented the house to Joseph-Edouard Cauchon (1816-85). Lawyer, newspaper editor and politician, Cauchon had been mayor of Quebec City, and Commissioner of Crown Lands and Commissioner of Public Works before being appointed as first Speaker of the Senate in 1867. He later sat in the House of Commons, and in 1877 he left Ottawa to become Lieu-tenant-Governor of Manitoba. It is thought that the house was named Stadacona Hall by Madame Cauchon, in honour of Cauchon's city of origin, Quebec, which was called Stadacona by the Indians. Sir John A. Macdonald inhabited the house while he was leader of the Opposition. Early in the twentieth century the house was rented to Sir Frederick Borden (1847-1917), Minister of Militia and Defence in the Laurier government. Later tenants included the ambassador of France, before the present French Embassy was constructed on Sussex Drive. In 1938 the house was purchased by the government of Belgium to serve as an ambassadorial residence. Considerable effort and expenditure have been made on the part of the Belgians to maintain the house in its present, excellent condition.

As its exterior suggests, Stadacona Hall has a long, rambling interior layout, with rooms of many different sizes and shapes arranged informally along a central corridor. The multiplicity of room sizes and shapes is reflected on the exterior, which is a picturesque mass of projecting wings, steep roofs, prominent gables, deep eaves, and decorative chimney stacks. There are plenty of windows in a variety of shapes, set in walls that are exaggeratedly rough. Numerous additions have been made over the years, and most of them are sympathetic to the whole. The main rooms boast truly superior plaster mouldings in the cornices, rosettes, and fireplace overmantles, as well as corinthian columns and a fine staircase. The best vantage point from which to see this house is the pathway that borders the western edge of the property.

45

Laurier House

335 Laurier Avenue East
1878

Laurier House was built in 1878 for a jeweller named John Leslie. Sir Wilfrid Laurier took up residence in 1897 when the house was purchased for him by the Liberal Party. As Prime Minister from 1896 to 1911 and thereafter Leader of the Opposition, Laurier resided here until his death in 1919. Lady Laurier remained here until she passed away in 1922; the house was then bequeathed to Mackenzie King, who was Prime Minister for most of the twenty-seven years that he resided here. He maintained his principal office in the attic storey of Laurier House, rather than on Parliament Hill, so one might fairly say that the country was run from this house for many years.

Built in the golden era of Sandy Hill's development in the last quarter of the nineteenth century, Laurier House is significant for its architecture as well as its historical associations. With its mansard roof and segmentally arched window openings, it is a good example of the Second Empire style as it was used in domestic architecture. Aside from the mansard roof,

Laurier House in the 1950s.
(National Archives)

other details of the style include segmentally arched openings such as seen here. Pale yellow brick was popularly used in Canada as part of the Second Empire Style for the effects of light and shadow that it helped to create. The Laurier House verandah is a good example of the elaborately turned and carved verandahs that were common to domestic architecture in Canada in the second half of the century. Only recently was it necessary to replace the original slate roof, which had lasted over one hundred years.

King willed the house to the nation. In memory of two remarkable figures in Canadian history, Laurier House was created a national historic site and is open to the public as a museum. One room has been consecrated to Prime Minister Lester B. Pearson, although he had no connection with the house.

Laurier House maintains its interior room arrangements and decoration, and it is furnished much as it would have been during the residency of its two most distinguished tenants, Sir Wilfrid Laurier and William Lyon Mackenzie King.

46

Cartier Square Drill Hall

Laurier at Canal
1879

The Drill Hall in 1890.
(National Archives)

It is difficult nowadays, when Canada and the United States boast about sharing "the world's longest undefended border", to imagine an era in which we were uneasy adversaries. The 1860s was an era of tension in British North America, and several incidents between Britain and the United States, including the Fenian raids into Canada, threatened to lead to serious hostilities. By the time of Confederation in 1867 tensions had eased somewhat, and in 1872 the British garrisons departed from Canada, leaving the fledgling Department of Militia and Defence to provide for the defence of the young Dominion. After the British withdrawal, the federal government started an ambitious program to construct drill halls in all of the strategically significant parts of the country, to provide storage and drill space for the Active Volunteer Militia.

The Cartier Drill Hall was one of three major drill halls constructed in the 1870s in Ontario (London and Toronto were the others). It was the first permanent drill hall and is the oldest extant city drill hall in Canada. The hall was designed by the Department of Public Works, under the direction of the first Chief Architect, Thomas Seaton Scott, and situated on land once owned by Lt. Col. John By. The building houses the Governor General's Foot Guards and the 43rd Battalion, two volunteer regiments who have continued to use the building for more than a century. A master of the Italianate style of architecture, T.S. Scott had his staff produce a fine adaptation of the style to the purposes of a drill hall. The long, round-headed windows light a high interior space. Corner towers reminiscent of Italian campanile frame the main facade. Inside, there was sufficient space, bridged by wooden trusses, that the thirteen companies that made up Ottawa's volunteer militia in the 1870s could drill in an unobstructed area. The sobre facade of the building was probably the result of the limited funds available for the project, but the design is both balanced and lively. Although Cartier Square has been reduced in size as a result of recent urban developments, it remains an excellent open space for large public events. The Governor General's Foot Guards, which perform the ceremonial duties at the opening and closing of Parliament, have become a major tourist attraction. The changing of the guard ceremony in the summer months begins at Cartier Square.

The Drill Hall has undergone remarkably few changes over the past century. In 1981, renovations improved the safety of the hall and replaced its roof. The brick walls were sand-blasted and protected with a coating of paint. Despite minor changes, the Cartier Drill Hall stands today much as it was in 1879.

47

Lisgar Collegiate

49 Lisgar Street
1874; 1892

Lisgar Collegiate has had a complicated building history, as its rather complex design shows. In 1872-74, Montreal architect W.T. Thomas was commissioned to design a school for the Dalhousie District Grammar School, which until this date had been housed in a variety of unsatisfactory rental properties. Thomas erected a modest yet handsome Gothic Revival school. By 1892 the school population had expanded so much that an extension was required. In that year an addition was

Lisgar Collegiate, circa 1875-80.
(National Archives)

put on the front, designed by Ottawa architect James Mather, that brought the building up flush with Lisgar Street. In the very next year, fire destroyed the building. Mather was engaged to rebuild the structure using the 1892 plans. Over the years the school population continued to grow, necessitating further additions. A new east wing opened in 1903, again designed by Mather; and a new west wing opened in 1908, designed by E.L. Horwood. In 1951 a gymnasium was erected across the street and connected to the main building by a tunnel.

Lisgar Collegiate illustrates well the eclecticism of late nineteenth century Gothic Revival design. The Gothic Revival details are clearly discernible in the pointed windows, crenellation and turrets. The overall composition of the central and oldest portion is based upon the designs of English university buildings that date from the later Middle Ages. The mansard roof is a feature borrowed from Second Empire design, and it was frequently combined with the Gothic Revival style in Ottawa public buildings, especially the East and West Blocks of the Parliament Buildings, and the Ottawa Teachers' College nearby (see Number 48).

In the mid-1970s the Ottawa Board of Education made plans to tear down Lisgar Collegiate. The protest staged by the school's staff, students, alumni and various heritage groups persuaded the Board to keep the building and to restore it. Lisgar has since been designated under the Ontario Heritage Act.

48

Ottawa Teachers' College

Elgin and Lisgar Streets

Moral improvement was a key theme of Victorian Canada, and education was considered the essential first step in the advancement of the nation as a whole. The Ottawa Teachers' College had its origins in this age of improvement as the Province of Ontario sought to bring into effect a free, universal, high-quality educa-

Teachers' College.
(National Archives)

tional system with competently-trained teachers as its essential base. Although municipalities constructed many new school buildings as a result of reformist impulses, the Ottawa Normal and Model School, or Ottawa Teachers' College, was the only building constructed by the province itself. It alone remains of the teachers' facilities built in Ontario in the nineteenth century.

The College was constructed in 1874-75 by the Belleville contractor, John Forin, based on the designs of the prominent Toronto architect, W.R. Strickland. It originally stood on an expansive, shady, four-acre site on what was then the fringes of the city. The Elgin Street portion was constructed first, and two later additions, in 1879 and 1891-92, provided for a model school (for practice teaching) and an assembly hall with additional class-rooms. In 1919 a further renovation added the 85-foot chimney and changed the exterior windows.

Twentieth-century encroachments have altered the originally sylvan setting of the college, but the exterior of the building largely retains its original lines. After passing from the province to the federal government to the University of Ottawa to the regional government, renovations will shortly result in a new life for the building.

The persistent influence of the Parliament Buildings in public design may be seen in the facade of this building. The similarities may be found in the composition of a centre section with flanking projecting pavilions, and the use of the steep, mansard roof. The Teachers' College still has a slate roof (recently restored), which the Parliament Buildings have lost. The architectural details are cheerfully eclectic: round-headed Italianate windows, accompanied by pointed Gothic voussoirs, set within a composition that is fundamentally classical in its symmetry and regularity.

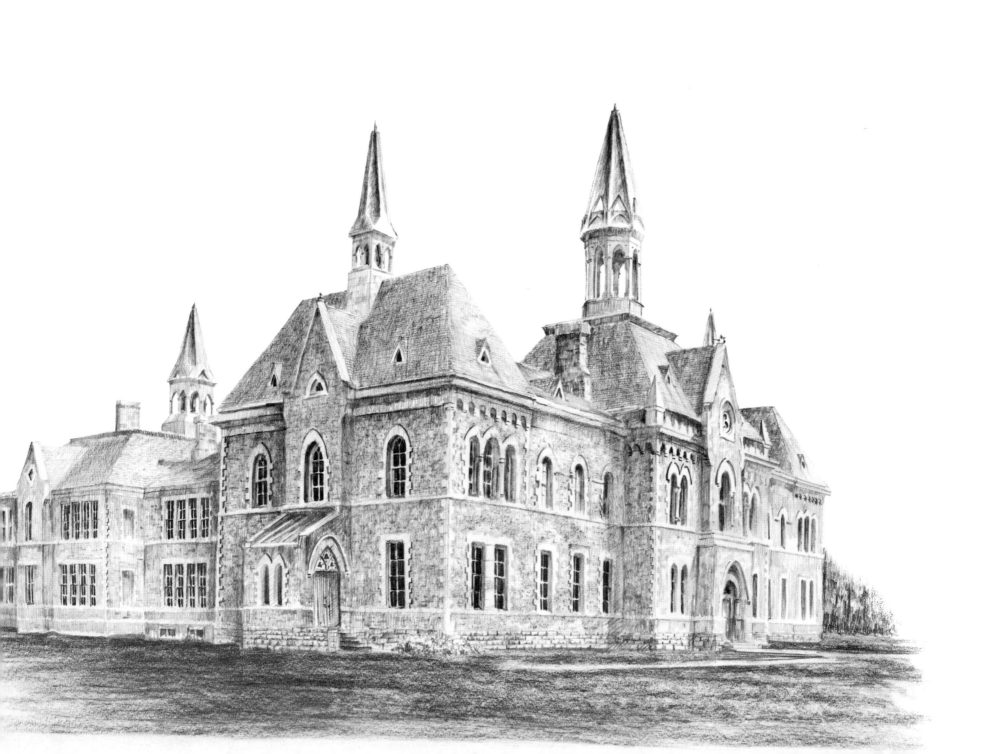

49

Thomas Birkett House

306 Metcalfe Street
1895

T.M. Birkett Residence.
(National Archives)

This house was built in 1895 for Thomas Birkett, a hardware merchant. Birkett was mayor of Ottawa from 1891 to 1899, and a member of Parliament from 1902 to 1924. The house has served as the Japanese Embassy, and as headquarters for the Boy Scouts of Canada. It is now the headquarters of the Heritage Canada Foundation.

It might be more accurate to describe this house, also known as "Birkett Castle", as fanciful, rather than tasteful. One does not often find crenellation — the cuts along the roofline meant to give medieval archers a protected view against assaulting forces — on houses in nineteenth century Canada. The house has a rather tight design, and the round and rectangular towers project only slightly form the flattish facade. Contrasting white stone and ornamental brickwork further adorn the surfaces. The interior woodwork and stained glass are a delight to the eye.

50

Hollywood Parade

103-113 James Street
1892-93

Originally the land upon which this building sits was acquired by Lieutenant Colonel John By in 1832. By's estate was sold in 1876 to a group of real estate speculators, who in turn sold this lot to one James Corry in 1892. A contractor by trade, Corry probably began construction on the Hollywood Parade the very next year. Until 1949 the building appears to have been owned by absentee landlords who leased out the units individually. In 1949 the units were sold off. Despite some modernizations, this terrace house is in very close to its original condition.

The architect of the Hollywood Parade borrowed shamelessly from almost every revival style of the nineteenth century in order to create this fanciful and entertaining design. The details include wide voussoirs from the Romanesque Revival, horseshoe arches that are Moorish in origin, segmentally arched windows and corbels that are Italianate, and features along the roofline that defy categorization. Executed primarily in red brick, Hollywood Parade has keystones and springing stones of a contrasting pale colour of stone, marble columns, terra cotta decorative panels, and extensive metal work along the roof. Stained glass panels fill the upper portions of each window.

The row consists of six identical units, the doors grouped in pairs beneath generous arches. Each unit contains a living room, dining room and kitchen on the ground floor, and five bedrooms on the second floor. The interior trim is plainer than the exterior might lead one to expect. Mouldings are attractive but simple, and the mantelpieces are finely carved.

Attached houses, or townhouses, became more common in Canadian cities towards the end of the nineteenth century. They appeared as a result of the rising cost of land in built up areas. French Canadians had long been accustomed to attached housing, especially in densely packed cities like Montreal and Quebec City. English Canadians, however, still preferred detached houses, each with its own patch of garden.

51

Aberdeen Pavilion

Lansdowne Park
1898

The Aberdeen Pavilion in 1904.
(National Archives)

In the nineteenth century, county fairs were held on a rotating basis in the fall in various Ontario towns. Originally these rural fairs gave farmers and small tradesmen a chance to congregate, trade information, and advertise their wares. The provincial government actively supported rural fairs because they helped farmers learn new farming techniques. At first, temporary, knock-down structures and tents served the purpose adequately. As these fairs grew in popularity, with industry and other groups wanting to participate, permanent sites and permanent buildings had to be created. After several years of participating as a temporary site for travelling provincial exhibitions, the city of Ottawa decided to create a permanent annual

exhibition, beginning in 1888. Within a decade the Central Canada Exhibition became so successful that larger, permanent buildings were needed. Participants agitated for, and received, the Cattle Castle (now the Aberdeen Pavilion), built in 1898 by local architect Moses C. Edey.

The ideal exhibition building had to have large, unimpeded interior spaces, good light and ventilation, easy ingress and egress, and fireproof materials. Moreover, the construction had to be fast and cheap. Edey's design called for a light-weight steel frame covered with pressed metal plates and large areas of glass. Inside there is a large, airy space with few support members to interfere with the use of the building for exhibition space. Extensive windows provide ample natural light and the clerestory along the roof aids the updraft of air, so important in a livestock building. The design is fun as well as functional, as a fair building should be. The ends and the side entrances have wide doors to allow large crowds to move freely. The doors are framed by fanciful turrets and cupolas, pediments and pilasters, all painted in festive colours. A central dome crowns all.

The Dominion Bridge Company of Montreal, one of the country's principal contractors in metal frame construction, put up the building in just two months. It was named for Governor General Lord Aberdeen, who was keenly interested in agricultural education. As the earliest surviving example of the steel frame exhibition building, the Aberdeen Pavilion has been designated an historic site by the City of Ottawa, and it is also a national historic site.

52

Echo Bank

700 Echo Drive
ca. 1865

Echo Bank was, at the time of its construction, a considerable distance from the centre of town. It was built as a suburban villa, and had a splendid view of the canal and the surrounding countryside. Despite its symmetry it has some of the picturesque features considered desirable in a house of this type. Notice the steep roof, deep eaves with decorative beams, bargeboards in the centre gable, and the pleasing contrasts of rough stone and smooth stone. There is one small pointed window in the gable.

The original owner of Echo Bank left his mark on the city of Ottawa. Colonel George Hay was president of the Bank of Ottawa, active in many local charities, and an alderman on city council. It was Hay who suggested the name "Ottawa" when the counsellors of Bytown were looking for a more dignified name for a city of growing pretensions. Hay is also thought to have been the designer of the City of Ottawa shield of arms. Echo Bank was rented briefly to the Cuban Embassy, but repeated bomb threats led the Cubans to erect a more secure structure elsewhere.

Echo Bank in 1896.
(National Archives)

53

Billings Estate

2100 Cabot Avenue
1828

The Billings Estate in 1925.
(National Archives)

Shortly before work began on the Rideau Waterway, a number of settlers had taken up residence in the Ottawa area. The nature of these earliest properties shaped the growth of the village that was to become Bytown. Lumberman Philomen Wright situated himself in Hull, and partly for that reason much of the lumber industry grew up there. Louis Besserer owned the land that became Sandy Hill, and he was responsible for its subdivision into residential lots. Nicholas Sparks owned the land on and around the street that bears his name. As his property was so close to military and later government buildings, it was natural to develop it for commercial purposes.

Development of the Billings Estate did not take place until this century, since it was well outside the city limits. Of New England origins, young Braddish Billings (ca. 1783-1864) came to the Ottawa area to work first as a lumberman for Philomene Wright. He abandoned lumbering for farming, and soon acquired an 800 acre parcel of land some 4 miles south of Bytown. This made him the first white settler of Gloucester township. In 1828 Billings began construction of the lovely Billings house, which remained in the family's hands until the 1970s. The farmland was sold off earlier, most of it going into the post-World War II housing developments nearby.

The white clapboard house suggests Billings' New England roots. Originally the house consisted of the middle two and a half storey section, which has a centre door and a central hall plan with 2 rooms to each side of the main passageway. The one storey wings to either side were added later. The symmetry of the elevation, the evenly spaced openings, and the gentle pitch of the roof reflect the influence of British classicism on vernacular architecture throughout North America at this time. The casement windows are typical of French Canadian architecture.

In the twentieth century there was a fashion for structures designed in imitation of eighteenth century classically-influenced buildings. This fashion led to the construction of many new buildings in this imitative style, and many existing structures were remodelled to suit the new taste. For this reason dormers were added to the roofline and dentils added to the eaves; neither of these features was commonly used in the early nineteenth century when the Billings house was constructed. The effect was to make the building rather more "New England" than it had originally been.

In 1974 the city of Ottawa acquired the Billings house and nine adjacent acres. Also surviving on the estate are a dairy, smoke house and gate house. All have been carefully restored and are open for public enjoyment. In 1983 the Billings Estate was declared a National Historic Site.

54

Fleet Street Pumping Station

Fleet Street Pumping Station
1874

The Pumping Station in 1898.
(National Archives)

Thomas Coltrin Keefer in 1869.
(National Archives)

The availability of fresh water is one of the features of twentieth century urban life that is generally taken for granted. But where does the fresh water come from?

For much of the nineteenth century, Ottawa was without a water system, as were most of the cities and small towns of Canada. Threat of fire was the motive for creating a water system, and in the early 1870s the

City of Ottawa contracted with the prominent civil engineer, Thomas Coltrin Keefer to do for Ottawa what he had already accomplished in Hamilton, Toronto and Montreal. The final result was a work of genius, which capitalized on the nearby Ottawa River to create a water system powered by a pumping station operated by hydraulic energy. In 1874 the Fleet Street Building, illustrated here, was erected. It remains in use today.

This pumping station is much as it was in the nineteenth century. The original mansard roof was replaced by a full second storey during one of the many expansions in pumping supply, but a renovation in the 1980s has endeavoured to capture faithfully the atmosphere of the building as it was at the turn of the century.

Fresh, filtered water comes to the Fleet Street Station from the Lemieux Island filtration plant, constructed in 1932 to provide Ottawa with a fresh water supply. Water to power the hydraulic pumps comes from nearby Nepean Bay in the Ottawa River. Although the original aqueduct is no longer in use, a second aqueduct, completed in 1912, still powers the pumps. After generating the fresh-water pumps, the spent water then flows via a small ravine back to the Ottawa River near the National Library.

Although there have been alterations made to the environment around the pumping station and to the building itself, one can still appreciate the quality of the design. The original portion consists of the ground floor storey up to the original cornice. The great height of the ground floor was needed to accomodate the pumping machinery inside. The interior was generously lit by paired windows with segmentally arched openings. At one time the building had a mansard roof, which has since been replaced by the present extra storey, executed in materials and in details similar to the lower storey.

55

The Mill

This building, originally a sawmill and a gristmill, is the oldest surviving structure of what was once an extensive complex of industrial buildings, encompassing both the Ottawa and the Hull sides of the Ottawa River and the islands in between. Before the arrival of settlers to this area, the magnificent Chaudiere Falls were a daunting obstacle for the fur brigades travelling inland. In 1800, Philomene Wright settled on the north shore of the Ottawa River in what is now Hull, and for him the falls represented a handy source of power to drive his mills. Other mills were built soon after on both sides of the river, including this one, erected in 1842 by Philip Thompson and John Perkins. The whole of the site was soon taken over by the E.B. Eddy Paper Mill. The Falls have since been harnessed for electricity, and it is difficult to appreciate the natural beauty of the spot for the collection of dam and industrial structures that obscure it. The complex of buildings, however, has its own interest. Behind the Mill is a timber slide dating from the era when log booms still filled the Ottawa River at this point.

Mills were the industrial and economic foundation of many Ontario towns and cities. Settlers established farms as close as they could to streams or rivers. These waterways not only provided the water power necessary to grind grain and saw lumber, but also provided the transportation route out to markets in Great Britain and the United States. The 1840s and 1850s were the heyday of the Ontario mill. Grain exports to Britain grew enormously, as did timber exports to the United States. It was only at the end of the century, with the opening up of the Canadian West, that these mills lost their raison d'etre.

Mill architecture was a straightforward construction of a building to a purpose. What was needed was a large interior space, well-ventilated and well-lit by many windows, and solid construction to withstand constant vibrations.

In 1968-71 the National Capital Commission restored the Mill, and it now houses a restaurant.

56

The Carbide Mill

Victoria Island
1899-1900

The solid, imposing structure once known as the Ottawa Carbide Mill had its origins in 1892, when Thomas Leopold Willson discovered a manufacturing process for calcium carbide, a substance that, when ignited, permitted the release and burning of acetylene gas. Almost at once this new, bright gas, nearly twenty times more luminous than natural gas, was regarded as the future light source for cities, homes and factories.

Victoria Island was an excellent location for a carbide mill, since a substantial amount of hydraulic or electric power was required to produce carbide from its constituent elements, lime and charcoal. Unfortunately, it was also a dangerous production process. In 1899, the Dominion Carbide Company in Ottawa was complete-

ly destroyed by fire after an explosion. The Ottawa Carbide Company, an affiliate of the Bronson Company, was then formed to take advantage of the temporary vacuum in carbide supply. It constructed the Ottawa Carbide Mill on Victoria Island between 1899 and 1900. Despite a relatively recent fire, the building still stands, a testament to the solidity of its construction techniques.

Between 1892 and 1910 carbide enjoyed its glory years, but electric light soon proved to be more efficient and less dangerous. Carbide was relegated to industrial uses only, and in 1911 the carbide mill was sold to the federal government, which used the building for a variety of warehousing purposes.

Carbide Works.
(National Archives)

57

Heney House

150 Richmond Road
1830s

Syringa Cottage on the Richmond Road, home of John Heney (demolished).
(City of Ottawa Archives)

Like many early houses in the Ottawa area, the Heney house distantly suggests both French and English influences. The general symmetry of the house recalls faintly its roots in British classicism. The casement windows and mansard roof (which probably dates from the 1870s) are characteristic of Quebec architecture. This building was built as a double for farm labourers.

Behind the building's modest exterior lies an association with a colourful episode in Ottawa's history. The structure was built by one Peter Aylen (1799-1868), an Irishman who had arrived in Canada in 1815. After working in the area as a labourer, Aylen purchased property from Ira Honeywell and settled down to farming and lumbering. He quickly acquired extensive timber interests in the valley.

Aylen became a leader of the Irish community. After the canal was finished, hundreds of Irish workers found themselves unemployed. There was seasonal work to be had as oak cutters (chêneurs — anglicized to shiners), but in this work they were in competition with the French Canadians who had hitherto dominated the lumber and timber trades. The Shiners committed numerous assaults in an attempt to intimidate the French into leaving the valley. Aylen encouraged the Shiners' activities, and even participated in an assault upon Daniel McMartin, a lawyer from nearby Perth. The violence continued unhindered, since no civil police force existed to stop it. Only in exceptional circumstances were the garrison troops called out, as the protection of government property was their sole responsibility. Murder, rape, assault and rioting continued, and the perpetrators were led by Aylen.

In 1837, a Rebellion broke out in Upper Canada. Although the strife was brief, many local residents took up arms to help suppress the Rebellion. Once the townsfolk were armed and organized, Aylen quit the cause and slipped across the river to Aylmer which, being in a different jurisdiction, put him beyond the reach of the legal actions outstanding against him. Curiously, Aylen settled down to a life of quiet respectability, and he died a pillar of Aylmer society.

The house on the Richmond Road was probably built for the labourers on Aylen's farm. In the 1860s Aylen sold the property to John Heney, who lived across the street in a much larger house that burned down long ago. No doubt it was Heney who added the mansard roof to enlarge the living space. Heney was also an Irishman, but a man of very different character from Aylen. Trained as a shoemaker and saddler, Heney went into the retail business, and also made himself wealthy in real estate. He served as an alderman for the city of Ottawa from 1857 to 1879.

The house stood in shabby neglect for some years, until purchased recently by an enlightened owner. Stucco that had been applied in the 1930s was removed, and the structure has been sympathetically restored.

58

Nepean Town Hall

345 Richmond Road
Westboro
1896

Town hall design in Ontario in the early part of the century was fairly simple. All that was needed was a structure large enough to accommodate an assembly room and perhaps one or two offices. Some communities sensibly combined several functions under one roof, and one finds town halls built in conjunction with fire halls, markets, or even opera houses. Towards the end of the century, these functions became sufficiently specialized to make such combinations unsuitable, and so town halls were given over entirely to municipal government.

How artistically designed these buildings were depended entirely upon the ambitions of the community. Designed by the Ottawa architect M.C. Eddy, the Nepean Town Hall was constructed in 1896, a small but dignified public building that stood as testimony to the aspirations of a village now swallowed up by a growing City of Ottawa. Finished in rugged stonework, this finely-proportioned building has a varied roof-line and prominent dormers that lend it a certain picturesque quality, helping it adapt well to its site and its location beside a church.

59

Maplelawn

529 Richmond Road
1831-34

This handsome house is a fine example of the influence of British classicism on domestic design. Such designs have a timeless appeal. Here is a centre door placed on a symmetrical, five-bay wide facade. Slender casement windows are set in rough-cut limestone masonry with trimmed door and window mouldings and corner quoins. A graceful Adamesque elliptical arch crowns the door. Overall is a hip roof framed by end chimneys. While the general composition reflects a taste for British classicism, the casement windows and hip roof are features particularly favoured in Quebec architecture and commonly found in the Ottawa Valley.

Inside there is a centre hall plan with two rooms on each side of the hall. Though the mantelpieces and much of the interior trim have been removed, enough remains to retain the beauty of the rooms. The staircase features a delicately turned nested newel post. Six-panelled doors and boxed window and door trim survive from the earliest date of construction.

Renovations have been made frequently to the house, but most have been sympathetic to its original character. The mantelpieces were replaced in the 1870s by carved oak ones more in the current fashion. In 1936 a rear addition, which once housed a summer kitchen and a farmhands' dormitory, was replaced with the present two and a half storey stone structure. The stonework of the new addition harmonizes with that of the main block but the mansard roof is a bit out of keeping. At the time this addition was put on the kitchen was moved into the main block of the house and a tradesman's entrance opened up into it. It is not known who designed Maplelawn, but the stonework attests to the fine quality of work done by the stonemasons who were drawn to the region by the Rideau Waterway project.

As remarkable as the house itself is the walled garden at one side. Walled gardens have existed in Europe for centuries, valued for the sense of sanctuary that they provide, and for the microclimate that they create, favourable to the cultivation of delicate plants. While walled gardens were common in Britain they were rare in Canada, and few others are known to survive from this early period. Such an extensive garden was meant to be useful as well as ornamental: herbs, fruit trees, berries and vegetables were cultivated here along with flowers and bushes.

Maplelawn was the centrepiece of an extensive 200 acre farm, laid out along the road that connected Bytown with the village of Richmond. The village of Nepean (now a suburb of Ottawa called Westboro) grew up just to the east of the house. Only two families have lived here, the Thomsons and the Coles. The land was settled about 1818 by William Thomson, a gentleman of Scottish origin who had retired from the British army to farm. Thomson and his sons invested peripherally in the lumber trade, which was the reverse of the usual habit of working in lumber and doing a bit of farming on the side.

In 1877 the Thomson family sold the farm and house to Thomas Cole, whose principal interest was in lumber. A granddaughter of Cole, Mrs. Lloyd B. Rochester, was the last private resident of the house. The house was acquired by the National Capital Commission. At the time of writing, various plans are being discussed for the future use of the house, but any project undertaken will respect the historic character of the house and grounds.

60

Bingham-McKellar House

635 Richmond Road
1840s

A bit farther down the road is another lovely country villa, dating from the 1840s. The similarity with Maplelawn is clear: this is also a stone building with centre door and symmetrically placed windows. There are a few differences, such as the gable roof, the verandah, and the French windows. The French windows are particularly attractive, and they make the house relate more closely to the grounds.

During the early part of the nineteenth century, a new attitude towards buildings and their relationship to their settings began to influence architecture. This was called the Picturesque Movement. Tired of the formality of eighteenth century architecture and landscaping, certain British designers brought into vogue a taste for more naturalistic landscaping. Architects responded with house designs that made the house fit into its setting in a more integrated way, as though the house were an element in a landscape painting. French doors and verandahs, such as we see here, became fashionable; they were destined to make the transition between interior and exterior spaces less distinct. The Bingham-McKellar house retains its formality, while attempting something of this more relaxed relationship with the setting.

The Bingham-McKellar house has had a more difficult history than Maplelawn. Said to have been built by one of Thomson's sons, it passed though many hands. Archibald McKellar and John Bingham were farmers who owned the house later on. Early in this century columns and a pediment were added to the front; while very grand, this portico was too large for the scale of the house. Over the years the interior was almost totally destroyed. The house served as a radio station for a while. In the 1970s the grounds were given over to a townhouse development, and the contractor restored the house as well as surviving structural and archival evidence would allow. The portico was removed and replaced by the present front verandah, in imitation of the front verandah which was known to have existed as far back as the 1870s. A low wall facing the Richmond Road survives, and suggests something of the country villa atmosphere that once existed here.

The house has been designated under the Ontario Heritage Act.

61

Olde Forge

2730 Carling Avenue
ca. 1851

This log building stands isolated in a sea of modern development. It was originally a blacksmith shop, part of a cluster of structures on the Winthrop family property. In the 1930s the structure was rebuilt into its present form.

There are many types of log construction; the type seen here is perhaps the best known. Trees of sufficient length and girth were felled, squared, and laid one upon the other, dovetailed at the corner. Only for the very crudest barnyard structures were the logs left round and the bark unpeeled. One can clearly see here that a much better joint is created with squared logs, and they are much more easily chinked with a binding substance, usually straw and mud.

Contrary to popular belief, horizontal log construction was not the earliest form of construction that settlers in Canada used. The French brought a much more sophisticated system in which short, horizontal pieces of wood are slotted into evenly spaced vertical members. Then the whole was covered with planks to stiffen the frame and to insulate it. English colonists to the south preferred frame and half-timbering. It was not until the Swedes arrived in the mid seventeenth century that log construction appeared in North America. The log house was less draughty than the English frame house and therefore more suitable to a colder climate, and it required less skilled labour, an important consideration in a thinly populated colony. Log construction became widespread in the nineteenth century, coincidental with the settlement of Ontario; that is why the log building is such a common sight in rural Ontario. Log was used for many purposes: houses, farm buildings, churches, schools, inns, jails and many others.

While the log house has a certain rustic charm to our eyes, it was not much treasured by those who lived in it. Such buildings were never entirely windproof and were often infected with vermin. Once resources allowed, families abandoned their old log house to the pigs and built themselves something finer in timber, brick or stone. Barring a completely new house, the log was frequently disguised with some kind of sheathing — siding or brick, for instance. Many a renovator has been surprised to find log underneath something else. The fact that the renovators of the 1930s left the ground floor bare illustrates that the log cabin myth of the twentieth century had taken hold.

The City of Ottawa purchased the house in 1962 and it now serves as a community centre.

62

Moffatt House

Silver Spring Farm
3501 Richmond Road
1867

The Moffatt House was built by the Bearman brothers, who were second generation Ottawa Valley farmers. They chose this site for its good land, and for its location on the Richmond Road, linking Ottawa with the nearby settlement of Richmond (founded in 1818). The barns appear to date from the late nineteenth and early twentieth centuries. The interior of the house has been modified over the years, first by Dr. H.B. Moffatt in 1944, and more recently to make the building suitable as a group home for the mentally disabled. The farm is now run for the Ottawa and District Association for the Mentally Retarded; the farm is also well known for its spring water.

The Moffatt House is an especially handsome Gothic Revival villa. Built of random coursed limestone, the house features bold, peaked gables with sinuously cut bargeboard, a steeply pitched roof, and deep set window frames with their original label mouldings. Like rural villas of the era, the Moffatt House has a carefully planned relationship with its setting. It sits on a slight rise of land, and its deep verandah and large windows look out over a broad lawn with mixed trees arranged to enhance the appearance of the house. But this was also a working farmhouse as well as a gentleman's villa. Aside from the formal reception rooms, there was also a large kitchen wing, where much of the labour of a farm was carried out. Stylistically, the house is very like Earnscliffe (1855), but the Moffatt House has retained its exterior in closer to its original condition.

With its extensive barns built for hay, dairy cattle and horses, and with its accompanying land, the Moffatt House can still be appreciated as the working farm it once was. It is an island of green, sitting on a portion of the Greenbelt, sandwiched between the sprawling development encroaching from both directions.

Appendices

Tour Map

Most of the buildings illustrated in the book are in one of five areas: New Edinburgh, Sandy Hill, Lower Town, Centre Town and the Lebreton Flats. This map is only meant to help guide you once you reach these areas. Please use a commercially prepared city map to help you navigate around the city.

Buildings numbered 51, 52 and 53 are all south of the Queensway near Bank Street. The last six buildings in the book are all on Richmond Road and are easy to locate.

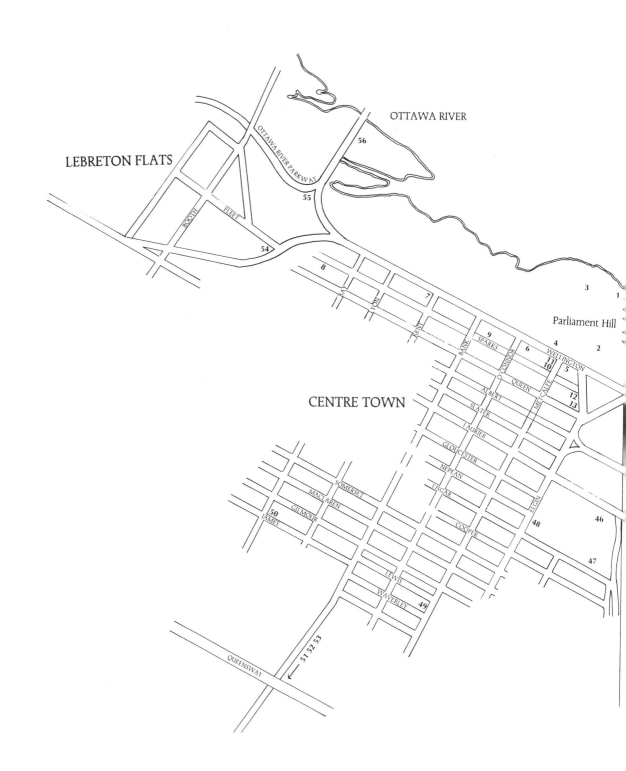

OTTAWA RIVER

22

SUSSEX

NEW EDINBURGH

JOHN
23
ALEXANDER
27
26
28
THOMAS
2425
RIDEAU GATE
CHARLES
30
31
MACKAY
UNION
CRICHTON
29

32

Rideau River

BRUYERE
ST. ANDREW
20
19
DALHOUSIE
CUMBERLAND
21
GUIGUES
16 17
ST. PATRICK
18
15
MURRAY
CLARENCE
PARENT
LOWER TOWN
YORK
14
GEORGE

NICHOLAS
WALLER
RIDEAU
35
33
34
BESSERER
STEWART
DALY
37
KING EDWARD
38
NELSON
39
FRIEL
36
LAURIER
CHAPEL
AUGUSTA
41 40
42
43
CHARLOTTE
45
44

SANDY HILL

List of Historically Designated Buildings in Ottawa

Provincial Historic Sites

Commissariat Building

Buildings Designated under the Ontario Heritage Act

Martineau Hotel
Valade House
541 Sussex
St. Alban-the-Martyr Anglican Church
City Registry Office
Carleton County Jail
Cartier Square Drill Hall
Central Chambers
Ottawa Teachers' College
Lisgar Collegiate Institute
Parliament Hill
Slater Building
Brouse Building
Stephens Building
93 Sparks
14 Metcalfe
Commissariat Building
Christ Church Cathedral
St. Andrew's Presbyterian Church
Langevin Block
Union Bank Building
Hollywood Parade
Aberdeen Pavilion
Birkett Castle
Fleet Street Pumping Station

National Historic and Architectural Sites

Aberdeen Pavilion
Billings Estate
Central Chambers
Parliament Buildings
Earnscliffe
Langevin Block
Laurier House
541 Sussex Drive
Ottawa Teachers' College
Grounds of the Parliament Buildings
Rideau Hall
Scottish-Ontario Chambers
Chateau Laurier
Bell Block
Daly Building
National Arts Centre
Central Post Office
Royal Canadian Mint
Former Railway Station
Rideau Canal

Rathier House
Archbishop's Palace
Earnscliffe
Donnelly House
LaSalle Academy
Notre-Dame Basilica
Henderson House
W.R. Latchie House
Fraser Schoolhouse
St. Bartholemew's Anglican Church
5 Rideau Gate
7 Rideau Gate
Minto Bridges
Rideau Canal
Echo Bank
Billings Estate
Bingham-MacKellar House
464 Besserer
Toller House
Besserer House
199-205 Daly
Patterson House
Philomene Terrace
Laurier House
Stadacona Hall
195 Nicholas
Heney House
Nepean Town Hall
Maplelawn
35 Mackay / 71 Thomas

Suggested Reading

History of the City of Ottawa:

Bytown: A Guide to Lowertown Ottawa (Ottawa: National Capital Commission, 4th edition, 1981).

Courtney C.J. Bond, Where Rivers Meet: An Illustrated History of Ottawa (Ottawa: Windsor Publications, 1984).

Robert W. Passfield, Building the Rideau Canal: A Pictorial History (Ottawa: Parks Canada and Fitzhenry and Whiteside, 1982).

Walking in Sandy Hill, Ottawa (Ottawa: Heritage Ottawa, n.d.).

Walking in New Edinburgh, Ottawa (Ottawa: Heritage Ottawa, n.d.).

John H. Taylor, Ottawa: An Illustrated History (Toronto: James Lorimer, 1986).

Harold Kalman and John Roaf, Exploring Ottawa: Ten Tours for Walking, Skating, Bicycling or Driving (Toronto: University of Toronto Press, 1983).

History of Canadian Architecture in the Nineteenth Century:

Margaret Carter, comp., Early Canadian Court Houses, (Ottawa: Parks Canada, 1983).

Marc De Caraffe, C.A. Hale, Dana Johnson, and G.E. Mills, Town Halls of Canada (Ottawa: Parks Canada, 1987).

Nathalie Clerk, Palladian Style in Canadian Architecture (Ottawa: Parks Canada, 1984).

Janet Wright, Architecture of the Picturesque in Canada (Ottawa: Parks Canada, 1984).

Leslie Maitland, Neoclassical Architecture in Canada (Ottawa: Parks Canada, 1984).

Mathilde Brosseau, Gothic Revival in Canadian Architecture (Ottawa: Parks Canada, 1980).

Christina Cameron and Janet Wright, Second Empire Style in Canadian Architecture (Ottawa: Parks Canada, 1980).

Leslie Maitland, The Queen Anne Revival Style in Canadian Architecture (Ottawa: Canadian Parks Service, 1990).

Glossary of Architectural Terms*

 Abacus, a slab on top of a classical column.

 Acanthus leaves, decorative foliage of a Mediterranean plant used in Classical ornament as in a Corinthian capital.

 Arch, a curved structure used in doorways, gateways, etc. as a support for the weight above it.

 Arcade, an arched passage.

Architrave, a main beam resting on top of a column or a moulding around a door, window or arch.

 Balcony, a platform projecting from a wall, enclosed by a railing or low wall.

 Balustrade, a low parapet, a row of balusters with rail used on a terrace or balcony.

 Bargeboard, decorated board on a gable edge or eaves line. Sometimes called gingerbread.

 Batten, strip covering a joint between vertical boards — sometimes ornamental.

 Belvedere, a roofed, but open or glazed structure usually located at the roof top of a dwelling.

 Blind arcade, line of arches or rectangles projecting slightly from a solid wall.

 Boomtown, false front masking a roof line.

 Bracket, angular support at eaves, doorways and sills.

 Buttress, mass of masonry or brickwork adding stability to a structure.

 Capital, crowning feature of column or pilaster.

 Casement, window with side hinged sashes.

 Chamfer, a bevelled corner.

 Clapboard, horizontal boards that overlap, applied as an exterior wall cover.

 Column, a freestanding vertical member supporting a horizontal member.

 Corbel, projection of stone, timber, etc. jutting out from wall to support weight or for decoration.

*Thanks to the Port Hope Branch of the Architectural Conservancy of Ontario, and to the Canadian Inventory of Historic Building of the Canadian Parks Service, for this glossary of architectural terms.

Corinthian, one of the three Grecian orders having bell-shaped capital with acanthus leaves.

 Cornice, ornamental moulding that projects along the top of a wall, pillar, or building, usually of wood or plaster, around the walls of a room, just below the ceiling.

 Corona, the greatest projection in a cornice designed primarily to throw off rain from the roof.

 Crenellation, wall with indented or notched brakes at the top, usually on the roof-line of buildings.

 Cresting, ornamental finish along the top of a screen, wall or roof, usually decorated and sometimes perforated.

 Cupola, small circular or polygonal dome on a roof.

 Dentils, small rectangular blocks, similar in effect to teeth, found in the lower part of a cornice.

 Dome, section of a sphere or other rounded shape often used as the crowning feature of a large building.

 Doric, the simplest order of Greek architecture. A plain capital, column and no base.

 Dormer, a window in a sloping roof.

 Drop, decoration hanging from a roof edge or gable end.

 Ears, lateral projections of the trim around the top of a classical opening.

 Eaves, lower edges of a roof projecting beyond the wall of a building.

 Entablature, detail of classic order; a wide and important horizontal moulded band on major buildings.

 Facade, the front of a building; side and rear walls also referred to as facades.

 Fanlight, a window, often semi-circular, over a door, with radiating glazing bars suggesting a fan.

 Fascia, (board) horizontal wooden board below the eaves, or one of the faces of an Ionic architrave.

 Fieldstone, stone used in a wall either in its rough, unfinished state or crudely shaped.

 Finial, pointed ornament at apex of gable or pediment of roof edge.

 Flemish bond, bricks laid with alternate headers and stretchers in each course.

 Fluting, a type of decoration consisting of long, round grooves — the vertical channelling on the shaft of a column.

 Fret, a cut-out ornament of geometrical composition.

 Frieze, member of cornice below fascia board and soffit, flat on wall surface, sometimes highly decorated.

 Gable, the enclosing lines of a sloping roof.

 Gallery, a long covered passage, partly open along one side.

 Gambrel, gable roof having a double pitch or two slopes on each side.

 Gingerbread, see Bargeboards.

 Glazing bars, small narrow pieces of wood, stone, or metal which hold panes of glass in a door or window sash.

 Gothic (window), narrow, vertical pointed window adapted from Gothic church design.

Gouge moulding, moulding decorated with shallow ornaments made with a gouge.

Half Timber, exposed wooden beams infilled with another material, usually stucco covered.

 Header bond, bricks laid to show only short ends in every course.

 Hipped roof, roof sloped on all four sides.

 Hood moulding, drip stone or label, projecting cover for window or door.

 Ionic, the second order of Greek architecture.

 Keystone, central stone of a masonry arch.

 Label, a projecting moulding by the sides and over the top of an opening.

 Lancet, a sharply pointed Gothic arch, resembling a lancet or spear.

 Lantern, a small structure raised above the roof, of various shapes with windows.

 Lintel, horizontal timber or stone over an opening that carries weight of structure above.

 Mansard, variation of hip roof with steep lower slope (which may be curved) and flatter upper section.

 Modillion, (bracket or console) a bracket or truss with scrolls at both ends.

 Moulding, a decorative band or strip of material used in cornices and as a trim around window and door openings.

 Mullion, a vertical member dividing window sections.

 Muntin, small, slender bars holding panes in a window.

 Ogee, design element formed by two convex arcs above two concave arcs.

 Oriel window, a bay window which is found on upper stories only.

 Palladian, arch-headed window flanked by narrower, shorter, square-headed windows.

 Panel, inset or outlined door division. An area of material within a frame or structure.

 Parapet, a low wall usually running along a roofline.

 Pediment, low triangle ornamenting the front or gable end of a building, door or window.

 Piers, square masonry supports; solid parts of a wall between openings.

 Pilaster, vertical, rectangular members projecting slightly from a wall.

 Plinth, projecting base of a building or statue.

 Portico, porch with pillars or columns.

 Quatrefoil, a panel divided by cusps into four sections. (Cusp, the point formed by the intersection of the foils in Gothic tracery).

 Quoin, a projecting corner stone at the angle of a building. From the French word, coin - corner.

 Rusticated, tooled (as on the surface of stone).

 Shingle, small square or polygonal pieces of wood used as a roof or wall covering.

 Sidelight, glazed panels adjacent to a door.

Soffit, under surface of eaves.

 Stringcourse, a moulding or projecting course running horizontally on a building surface.

 Trefoil, (three leaves), arch or window having a three-lobed opening.

 Soldier course, horizontal row of upright bricks.

Terra cotta, fine grade brick clay that lends itself well to decorative work.

 Turret, small tower, often containing stairs.

 Spandrel, the triangular space enclosed by the curve of an arch, or horizontal, dividing structural member between vertical piers on major buildings.

 Tie Rod, metal brace running through a building typing opposite walls together.

 Tynpanum, a flat wall surface within either a pediment or an arch.

 Spire, a tapering, polygonal form that crowns a church tower.

 Transom, horizontal bar between the top of a window or door and the structural opening.

 Veranda, a roofed porch.

 Stretcher, bricks laid lengthwise every course.

 Transom light, the section above a transom.

 Vermiculated, stonework in which the surface has been deeply carved with sinuous forms.

 Stucco, plasterwork used as an exterior surfacing material.

 Treillage, decorative, lacy trim, used on porches or garden features.

 Voussoir, a wedge-shaped stone used in arches.